 
13435 N.E. Whitaker Way, Portland, Oregon 97230
Phone (503) 254-9100

## DEDICATION

Dedicated to my daughter, Sara, who gave up a lot of her time with Mom so that I could finish this book. I hope that some day I can help make all of your dreams come true, too.

## ACKNOWLEDGMENTS

You know, it's really funny how two people from opposite ends of the country can meet and find out they're so much alike. Special thanks to Ralene, my kindred spirit here in Ohio.

## ABOUT THE AUTHOR

Art classes were not offered in her school when Kathie George was a child. So, she did not take a formal art class until after she was married - when her husband Michael signed her up for a college class as a surprise. Little did he know what he was in for! That art class changed their lives forever! From that moment on, any leisure time she could find was spent painting. In 1985, she quit her job and began to devote all of her time to her new career.

Currently, she teaches watercolor workshops across the United States. She has authored three books and is a member of the Florida Watercolor Society, the Ohio Watercolor Society, and the Southern Artists league.

For workshop information, or questions, write to:

Kathie George
310 East Van Emmon St.
Yorkville, IL. 60560

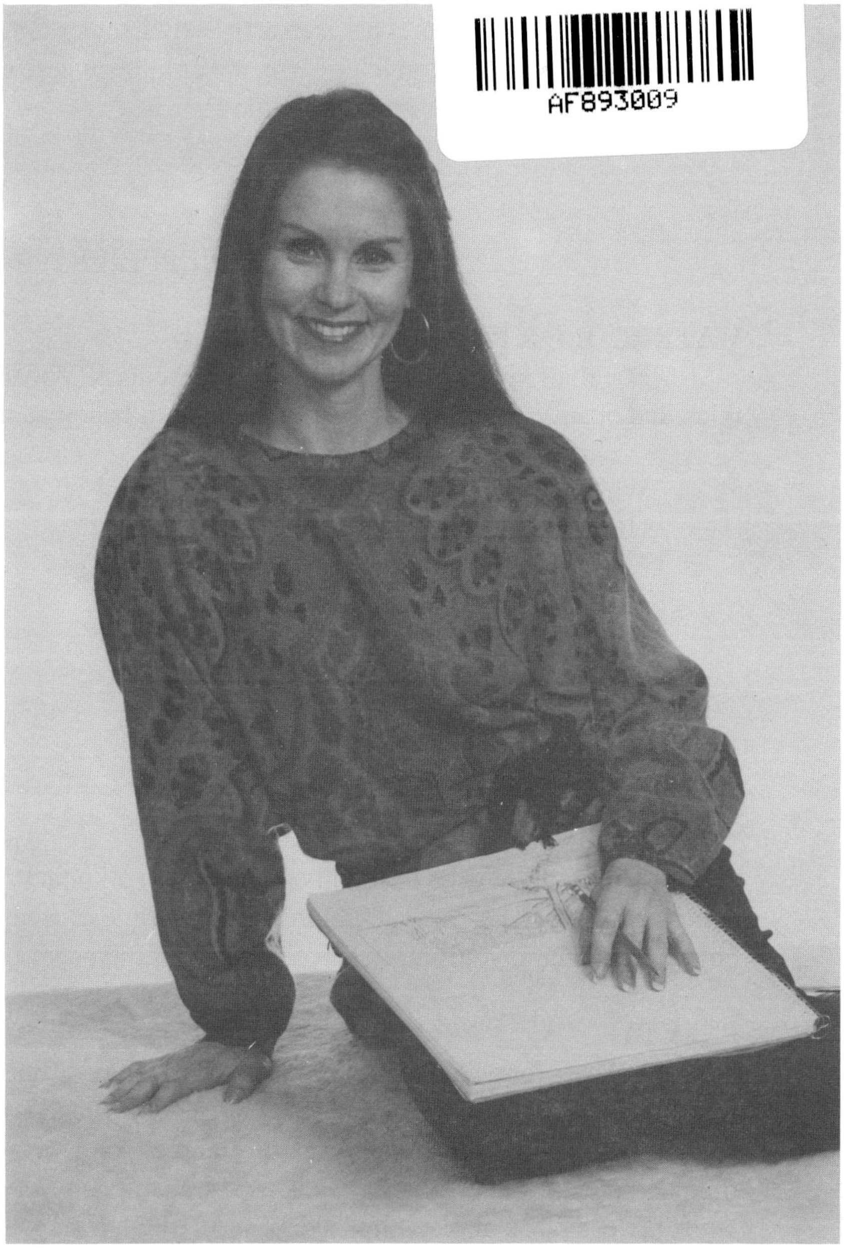

## INTRODUCTION

Watercolor is great fun! It's mysterious, too, because you don't always know exactly where the colors are going to go. If you're a beginner, that can be scary - right? Really, the mystery is part of the fun, and the beauty, of watercolor. That's where I come in. I'm going to lead you every step of the way! I'll tell you what to expect, what might happen, and if something should go wrong what you should do to correct it.

May I give you a tip about some things that have taken me years to learn? Believe it or not, an open mind and positive attitude have so much to do with a successful painting. Try not to be too hard on yourself - remember, you're learning! Enjoy the way the colors mix in the water, without always trying to do the mixing yourself. That seems to be the most difficult thing of all for students to do. Relax, and just let things happen. Remember, I was once just where you are now, starting out, a bit afraid but wanting to learn. That is exactly why I am so sure that you will be successful. Be stubborn, and determined! NEVER give up! You never know where a road can lead you. I wish you the best of luck and great discoveries on your journey.

## SUPPLIES

### WATERCOLOR PAINTS

For all of my paintings, I use tube watercolors (Winsor & Newton brand). Although the paint is thick and opaque when it comes from the tube, it becomes transparent when it is mixed with water.

| | |
|---|---|
| Winsor Blue | Cobalt Blue |
| Ultramarine Blue | Neutral Tint |
| Cadmium Red | Cadmium Orange |
| New Gamboge | Winsor Violet |
| Brown Madder | Alizarin Crimson |
| Raw Sienna | Burnt Sienna |
| Burnt Umber | Payne's Gray |
| Viridian | White acrylic or gesso |
| Prussian Blue | |

Those of you who have only painted with oil or acrylic may notice the absence of white watercolor from the palette. In watercolor, water, or white is used to lighten a color. Also, when you want an object to be white, you simply leave that part of the paper unpainted.

### PALETTE

Palettes for watercolor painting come in many different styles. Choose a palette that has a small well for each color you'll be using and a large, white central mixing area. You might also consider a lid so that it will be easy to take the palette and wet color with you wherever you go. If this is your first time to watercolor and you don't yet have a palette, any flat white surface will do: a butcher's tray, a white plate, a piece of plexiglass over a sheet of white paper. The reason the surface should be white is so that you'll be able to see the colors you are mixing. That is so important!

**BRUSHES**

Although I own many brushes, I find that I regularly use only three or four. They are:

Winsor & Newton Series 837, #8 Round, also #4 Round
Winsor & Newton Series 730, #1
Winsor & Newton Series 995, 1" Flat
Loew Cornell 7120 Rake, 1/2"

**A NOTE ABOUT BRUSHES**

The best flat wash brushes are made of red sable hair, which have excellent spring and bounce and hold large amounts of water. These brushes are expense however. So if you are a beginner you might try the Series 995 nylon bristle. The nylon bristle brushes are considerable less expensive than pure red sable and eventually, you may want to invest in red sable brushes. Watercolor is very easy on brushes. If you take good care of them, they will last many, many years.

**BRUSH CLEANING**

Keeping the brush clean will dramatically extend its life.

Here are some tips:
* When cleaning a brush made with natural hair, use cool water. Hot water will strip the natural oils from the hair.
*Always rinse the brush thoroughly in water to remove as much of the remaining color as possible.
*Allow the brush to dry upright or hanging downward.

**PAPER**

The paper on which you choose to paint your watercolors is very important. This is as important as your paints and brushes, especially as a beginner. Some students think that they should wait until they become "really good" before they use good paper, but that's not so! Just like using the correct brushes, learning to watercolor will be much easier if you use a good paper.

The paper I use, almost always, is Winsor & Newton 140 pound cold pressed watercolor paper. It is consistently top quality and tough, which means it will stand up to scraping, masking, scratching and all other torture techniques that are used to achieve paintings in this book. I particularly like this paper because of its whiteness and because it is made with vegetable instead of animal sizing, which means there is no odor when it is wet!

Another excellent paper is Arches 140 pound cold pressed paper. Both papers are acid free and will not become brittle or yellow with time. "Cold pressed" refers to the surface of the paper, which is slightly textured. Others surfaces are "hot pressed" which is smoother and "rough" which is more textured.

I never stretch my paper. For me, all that preparation takes all the fun out of painting. "Stretching " the paper refers to soaking it in water then fastening it onto a board while it is still wet. The paper expands when it is wet, and since it is taped down, cannot shrink back to it's original size. Therefore, it remains "stretched" out. This procedure removes the sizing and insures that the paper won't buckle when you get ready to paint on it. The buckling of the paper that occurs when the paper is not stretched does not bother me, I simply ignore it. Though it may be a bit bumpy when it dries, after it is matted it will straighten out. If the buckling bothers you, but you don't want to stretch your paper, try working on 300 pound cold pressed. This paper is more expensive, but is thicker and will not buckle.

Stretching the paper has been done since, well probably since the beginning of watercolor painting. A lot of artists insist on it - including many of the teachers that I have studied with. This is just what works well for me and makes my painting that much more enjoyable.

NOTE - never use oil products on your watercolor paper. That is, oil paint, alkyds or any products associated with them. Oil products deteriorate the paper!

**LIQUID MASKING PAPER**

Because of the transparent nature of watercolor, you can't paint light colors over dark. The light, white areas of a painting are always the clean, white paper itself. Therefore, there are times when you might like to carefully protect or save these white areas to be painted later in the painting process. This is where a liquid masking fluid is great.

There are several brands, and although they have different names, they all work the same way. This fluid is painted onto the paper and dries into a touch, rubbery film. It will not allow paint or any moisture to penetrate the paper. So, when it is removed later on, there will still be white paper underneath.

Masking fluid often has a color (pink, yellow) in the bottom of the jar. This is simply there to make it easier for you to see if after it's painted onto the paper. Just stir gently to mix in some of that color. Most brands of masking fluid cannot be shaken! That causes bubbles that will burst and leave a hole for the paint to seep through. Check the label to see if the brand you are using can be shaken.

To protect your brush from the masking fluid, you must first coat your brush with soap. This will protect the brush because latex will not stick to soap. Use a damp brush. Work it back and forth on a bar of soap until all of the water in the brush has been used up. Don't use soft soap because it's so thin it sometimes allows masking fluid to be absorbed by the paper. Be sure that the ferrule and the hairs of the brush are completely covered. Leave the soap in the brush while using the fluid, then rinse it thoroughly. A lot of artists prefer to use an old brush to apply masking fluid. I do not. When you paint on the latex you are actually painting white forms onto the painting, so I believe you should use a good brush that will enable you to paint neatly. When it is dry, you may paint over the area as if it were not there at all.

The paper must be dry before you take off the masking fluid. Never try to remove it from a damp surface. To erase the mask, you can use a rubber cement pick-up, or just rub off with a clean finger. Always be gentle whenever you erase anything so that you will not damage the surface of the paper!

**OTHER SUPPLIES**

Two water containers - one for clean water and the other to rinse the brush.

A support for the paper (can be pre-gessoed masonite, plywood or other non-absorbent material). This support should be at least an inch larger, all the way around, than the paper you are painting. You may choose to have more than one size, or just one large support that will work for all sizes of your paintings.

| | | |
|---|---|---|
| Masking Tape | Paper Towels | No. 2 Writing Pencil |
| Hair Dryer | Kneaded Eraser | Final Net Type Spray Bottle |

Scratchknife Blade (can also use X-acto knife)

## GETTING STARTED

Begin by squeezing out a generous amount of each color into the wells along the sides of your palette. Don't be stingy! Any color that is left over can be misted with a spray bottle and ready to go at your next painting session.

These beginning steps should be done before each painting. Hold the watercolor paper to the light and you will notice a watermark (trademark). If you can read this (if it's not reversed), then you are looking at the preferred side to paint on. This is the smooth side. It is perfectly all right to paint on the other side as well. (If you make a mistake, just turn it over and paint on the other side)! The "other" side will feel a bit rougher because the dimples will be reversed. Cut the paper to the correct size that is given at the start of each instruction. Then tape the paper to the support by placing one 2 or 3 inch long sections of tape on each of the four sides. If all the sides are taped completely around, the paper will buckle more because there is nowhere for it to expand but up.

Now position the working surface so that the top of the support is a bit higher than the bottom, perhaps an inch or so. This small slant helps the colors to blend together. You can use whatever you have around for this. I usually just stick my masking tape under the edge of the support.

### TRANSFERRING THE PATTERN

After the paper is cut and taped down, you may transfer the pattern, if so stated in the instructions. The very best way to transfer the pattern is to use a light box. If you don't have one, simply tape the pattern behind the watercolor paper on a window. You'll be able to see the pattern through the paper and trace it. Commercial graphite may also be used, but most commercial is "oily" and watercolor paint will run off of the traced lines. It is also very difficult to erase. So, if you're using commercial graphite, trace very lightly. Saral brand makes a good transfer paper because it contains no oil and will erase very easily.

It is preferable to make your own graphite by rubbing one side of a piece of good quality tracing paper with a soft graphite stick or woodless pencil. Rub with a crisscross motion until it is pretty well covered. Then dampen a piece of facial tissue with lighter fluid or rubber cement thinner, and using a circular motion, rub over the blackened surface. The graphite will smear at first, but if you keep rubbing it will soon become rather smooth looking. Before using it, be sure you have shaken all of the excess graphite from the surface to prevent it from soiling your watercolor paper.

Whichever method of transferring the pattern you choose, ALWAYS trace as lightly as you can. And, if you must erase, use only a kneaded eraser and a light touch. Never scrub or rub the paper as it is rather delicate. The surface can be damaged and once it is, it will not react in the expected way.

### MIXING YOUR PAINT

The proportions of paint and water will determine just how light or dark the color will be. To mix watercolor paint and water, start with a clean palette. (That is, the large white center section should be clean. You do not have to start with new color every time). Place about a teaspoon of clean water on the palette by dipping the brush into water, then transferring the water in the brush to the palette. Always use at least a teaspoon of water with every mixture. Next, dip the tip of the brush into the paint and carry it to the water. The resulting puddle is not ready to be painted onto the paper. After mixing, always test the color on a scrap of watercolor paper to be sure it is the correct value. If the color is too dark, just add more water. If it's too light, add more paint.

HINT: If you are mixing a very dark value, start with less water! Perhaps 1/4 teaspoon or so. This will enable you to reach a dark value faster. Then, if it's too dark, it's very easy to add a bit more water to the mix.

## THREE VALUE MIXING

All of the color mixes used for the paintings in this book are one of three values: light, medium or dark. A sample of this value scale is given for you on this page. Please match these three values on a scrap of watercolor paper and place it next to your palette. Then, TEST EACH AND EVERY COLOR you mix and compare it with the value scale to be sure it is the correct value. Remember that a light value has a lot of water and just a bit of paint. A dark value has much less water, but a lot more paint is in the mix!

HINT: When testing a color, do not use a brush fully saturated with the mix. The color will appear darker than it actually is. Rather, pick up a small amount of mix on just the tip of the brush; or, blot out excess water by touching a kleenex to the ferrule of the brush. Then test the color.

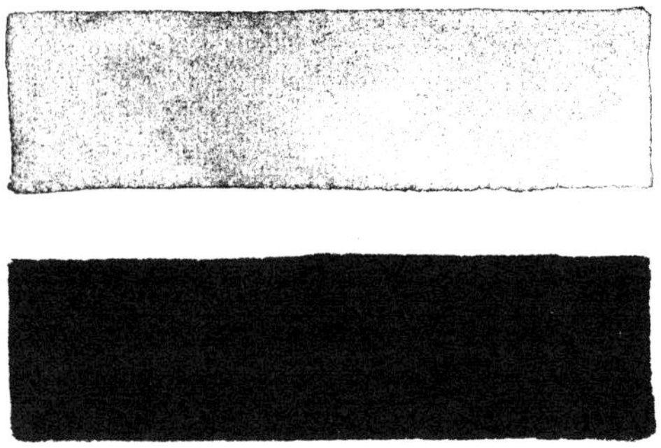

**LIGHT VALUE**

**MEDIUM VALUE**

**DARK VALUE**

## PAINTING TERMS

**WASH** - A thin layer of paint over the paper.
**TRANSPARENT** - Being able to see the white watercolor paper or another color through a wash.
**OPAQUE** - Non-transparent, any color that you cannot see through.
**NEGATIVE PAINTING** - To make an object appear by painting the background AROUND it, rather than the actual object itself.
**DRY OR WET?** - When painting with watercolor, the surface of the paper can be either dry or wet. Painting on a dry surface is sometimes call "wet or dry". When paint is applied to a dry surface. it will have a sharp edge and remain exactly where you put it.

Painting on a wet surface is called "wet on wet". The surface is wet if the paper has been sprayed or stroked with water, or if previously applied paint is still wet. Paint applied to a wet surface will blur and spread out. How much it spreads depends on exactly how wet the surface is. If it is very wet, the paint will sometimes "explode" outward. As the surface becomes less wet, the spreading will slowly decrease.

**DABBING** - This refers to a method of placing paint onto the paper by light, quick taps. Dabbing is always done on wet paper when you want the color to spread and soften. That is because each time you lift the brush it releases water from its tip. Follow instructions in this book carefully. Some instructions will say to "dab", others refer to:

**STROKING** - This refers to setting the brush onto the paper and moving it without lifting. Stroking can be done on dry or wet paper, but when done on wet paper, helps to control the color you are painting with. Remember that lifting the brush releases a little "puff" of water from the brush. Therefore, when you STROKE the color on and don't lift the brush you will retain much more control. Practice both of these methods to become familiar with what they do. Again, read the painting instructions carefully as to whether they call for "dabbing" or "stroking" a color.

**BLOW DRYING** - The appearance of a "blossom" is difficult to describe, but you will know it when you have one. They are caused when damp paper is suddenly flooded with water from an outside source. The water soaks into the paper, moving on until it reaches a spot that is dry enough to stop it. There the paint forms a starburst-looking area.

**SCRAPING OUT GRASS (What is that pointed brush handle for?)** - Some flat wash brushes are made with a great pointed handle. The Winsor & Newton series 995 is an example of this. This type of handle is great for scraping out grass or other textured shapes. This technique is used on "House on Fox Road" in this book.

In order for this technique to work, there must first be a surface of rich, wet color on the paper. Then tip the brush over a bit so that you will be using a bit of the side rather than just the very tip of the handle. Now pull up grass strokes. It's a very easy way to do grass if you hate painting liner grasses.

HINT: There are actually two types of grass that can be painted using this particular technique. They are both "pulled up" in exactly the same way, but the timing is different. If you pull up while the paper is very wet, the handle will make little indentations in the paper and the paint will be wet enough to run into those indentations. Therefore, you will get dark, thin grass. However, if you wait until the paper is just about to lose the shine to pull up the grasses, the pointed handle will work more like a squeegee and remove paint from the paper. Then you will get larger, lighter grasses. Both kinds are fun to do! Practice them both.

**USING A SCRATCH KNIFE BLADE** - Scratch knife blades are great for adding texture or reclaiming white paper. (You know, scratching out a mistake)! A scratch knife blade is a small blade that fits into a pen-like handle - it looks much like a crow-quill pen, but it is much sharper. Use the tip of the blade, but tilt it over on the side a little, don't stand it straight up on end. This way you can scratch the surface of the paper without gouging it as much. Carefully pick at the color. You can vary this technique from scratching paint off the surface to actually tearing the surface of the paper. An X-acto knife or razor blade may also be used.

**USING OPAQUE ACRYLIC WHITE** - Opaque color does not soak into the paper in the same way as transparent color, it appears to stand free on its own. Be aware of this and use it sparingly. Never use acrylic White where it will be surrounded by white paper. Over time, the paper will yellow slightly, but the acrylic will remain a very white spot on the painting. When using a liner and acrylic White, you will need to thin it slightly with water.

**SPATTERING** - Believe it or not, there is a technique to spattering. Never use color straight from the tube. Always thin it with water. How thin? Well, if you're spattering on dry paper, try a medium value color and if spattering on wet, use a dark value. Load the #8 round brush with the wash, then take out the extra water hitting the brush against a finger. The more water in the brush, the larger the drops. Another thing you should know about spattering is that the farther away the brush is held from the paper, the more the spatter will be spread out. So, if you want a neat, concentrated patch of dots, hold the brush in close to the paper. Until you gain control of this technique, always cover up everything that you don't want to be spattered. When you really get good at it, you can try to contour the spattering. That is, if you're painting a road, spatter horizontally to follow the contour of the ground, or spatter vertically over bushes and weeds.

A toothbrush can also be used for spattering. It works better for acrylic than watercolor, though. Toothbrush spatter is very fine.

**WORKING WET-ON WET** - Painting on "wet" paper is really the most challenging part of watercolor. Once you have this licked, you can paint anything! There are several lessons in this book which require you to paint onto paper wet either by water or with another color. When working wet-on-wet, follow these three simple steps:

1. Wet the paper evenly - no puddles and not dry spots.
2. Look for the shine. Unless otherwise instructed, do not paint unless the paper is shiny, and
3. Stop painting once it has lost the shine! Instead, dry the paper completely with a blow dryer and rewet it again to the shiny stage. THEN continue painting.

   Another tip is to avoid excess water in your brush strokes. There is already water on the wet paper. Think of wet-into-wet painting as "drybrush into wet".

**DRYBRUSHING** - this word is misleading. Actually, it is not the brush that's dry, it's the paper. A "Rake" brush, by Loew Cornell is great for drybrushing. A 1/2" size will be best for the size paintings in this book. A medium value paint works best for this type of drybrushing. If you do not own a "Rake", or cannot find one in your area, just use your #8 round brush. That's what I used for years before the "Rake" came along. Take the damp #8 round brush and fan out the bristles. (A synthetic brush does not work well). Do this by pinching the hairs at the ferrule until they form a sort of little fan brush. Then dip just the tips of the hairs into a color mix and lightly drag them across the surface of the paper. It should look like a sort of skid mark. If the brush hops across the grain of the paper, you need a touch more of the paper. It should look like a sort of skid mark. If the brush hops across the grain of the paper, you need a touch more of the mix in the brush. On the other hand, if the brush "closes up" when you load it, there's too much water in it. Blot it out, fan it out, then try again.

**BLENDING** - The edge of a still wet color can be softened by being stroked with a brush wet with clean water. Be sure to place your brush on the EDGE of the color only. If using a round brush, I like to pinch the bristles and fan them slightly. Note that an edge cannot be softened after the color has dried.

**BLOTTING** - When you're painting wet-on-wet, NEVER blot a mistake because a hard edge will then form along that dry spot. Instead, use a damp brush as a sort of vacuum cleaner to suck up unwanted water or paint!

**WETTING THE PAPER** - In this book, there are two ways in which you will be asked to wet the paper - either the entire sheet or a large section of the sheet, or an individual object within the painting. When wetting a large portion of the paper, use the 1" brush and long, swift strokes. Be sure that you get the edges of the paper. One dry corner can soakup a lot of moisture and make the paper dry a lot faster. And sometimes, by the time you've wet all the way to the bottom, the top will already be getting dry. So, check for a nice, even SHINE. No puddles and no dry spots. If the paper is not shiny, wet it again.

## COMMON PROBLEMS AND CORRECTIONS

**What if the Brush Drips a Spot of Color Somewhere I Don't Want It?**

Occasionaly this sort of thing happens. It can happen,of course, on dry or wet paper.

CORRECTION: If you are working on dry paper at the time, DO NOT BLOT. If you blot, you remove all of the moisture from the paper and it will "push" the color into the paper. First, flood the area with extra clean water, diluting the unwanted color as much as possible - then blot the lightened color off.

If you are working on wet paper, use a damp brush to suction up unwanted color and water.

**What's That Smell?**

Most watercolor papers have an unmistakable smell when they are wet. That comes from the sizing and is normal. There's an alternative. Winsor & Newton has a paper that is sized with vegetable sizing instead of animal sizing, and guess what - no odor!

**Washes Have a Hard "Rind" Edge and Are Thin in the Middle**

This usually happens when you wet a small area within the painting. It occurs when there is so much water on the paper that all of the color floats to the outside edge and collects there.

CORRECTION: Get into the habit of picking up any "pools" of water before they begin to dry. Use the tip of a damp brush to "vacuum" up the water.

**Large Areas Dry Too Fast**

Painting very large paintings, or even large areas within a painting, can be difficult for a beginner, so you're not alone! There are a couple of tips I can give you, however. First of all, always wet as much area as you can - not just the bare minimum. The more paper area that is pre-wet, the more drying time you have. Also, wet the sheet thoroughly to begin with and keep it wet as long as possible by working "around" the sheet - work color over the entire sheet, not just in one little spot. Remember, any time you add a wash to the paper you are also adding water and keeping the paper wet. In any case, don't ever forget that with a bit of practice you will get better and better. But give yourself time to learn!

**"Blossoms" or Watermarks (at the edge of the paper)**

These are usually caused when working wet-on-wet. The paper has been wet to the outside edge and water has collected there.

CORRECTION: After painting, always slide a paper towel under the outside edge of the paper to soak up the extra water that collects there. If you notice a watermark forming and the paper is still damp, try rubbing it off with a dry paper towel.

(Inside the Paper) - Remember how watermarks are formed: too much water introduced as the paper is drying. If there's a watermark forming inside the painting somewhere, chances are you came back into it with a wet brush and tried to add more color or "fix" a spot. (Come on, confess)! Accidental drops of water into damp areas can also cause this.

CORRECTION: First check for puddling. If there are puddles happening when you paint, wait until excess water has soaked into the paper before adding any other washes. The puddles should be gone, but the paper must still have a slight shine. AND, thicken up your color mixes by adding more paint.

**Puddles**

This can occur when adding color to wet paper or painting one wash on top of another. It may be that you wet the paper too much to begin with, but more likely you added the extra water when applying the color. Remember that each time you add a wash, you are also adding more water to the paper. You may think that you can darken an area by continuing to dab on washes when, in fact, the extra water is only diluting the color. Think of wet-into-wet painting as "drybrush in wet". Get the moisture onto the paper, then brush paint and as little water as possible with each stroke. See below for correction.

**Painting Always Turn Out Too Light**

If you can't seem to get an area dark enough this means one thing. YOUR PAINT MIXES ARE TOO THIN! This happens mostly when painting wet-on-wet, or when spattering large areas. If your washes dry too light -

CORRECTION: First check for puddling. If there are puddles happening when you paint, wait til excess water has soaked into the paper before adding any other washes. The puddles should be gone, but the paper must still have a slight shine. AND, thicken up your color mixes by adding more paint.

**"I Blend and Blend But It's Still Streaky"**

Many students think that the more they blend the color the softer their painting will be. Remember, stop blending before the paper loses it's shine. Once it has passed this point, each time you touch the brush to the paper it picks up a pit of color and makes a mark. So, you are actually painting on streaks instead of blending! However, if you stop blending while the paper is still shiny, there is enough water there to continue softening out the pigment for you. Relax, and let the water do some of the work for you!

**Masking Fluid Won't Erase Completely**

After erasing the masking fluid, if the paper feels oily or you have no control when painting that area, then the masking fluid has most likely penetrated the paper. There was probably too much water in the brush when you first applied the masking fluid. Reread how to apply it.

CORRECTION: The area is still paintable if you use very small amounts of paint/water in the brush. When masking fluid penetrates the paper it won't allow water/paint to soak in as it normally would. So, using less water should give you more control.

**My Finished Painting is Buckled**

Be sure to leave the painting taped down until it is completely dried. In any case, it will be fine after it has been matted. In extreme cases, carefully rewet the back side and tape down again until dry.

**"Snowflakes" at the End of Grass Strokes**

This occurs when painting on wet paper. Water is released from the brush every time it is lifted from the paper. So, when you make a stroke of color and lift the brush up, a spurt of water comes out and causes the paint to spread out.

CORRECTION: Stroke downward so that the snowflake occurs at the bottom where the grass is solid and thicker anyway.

**Paint Separates on Palette**

Certain grainy pigments will automatically separate on their own. That's their nature. Some of these are Yellow Ochre, Burnt Umber and Burnt Sienna when mixed with Ultramarine Blue. This doesn't hurt a thing. Simply stir the mixes gently before putting them onto paper.

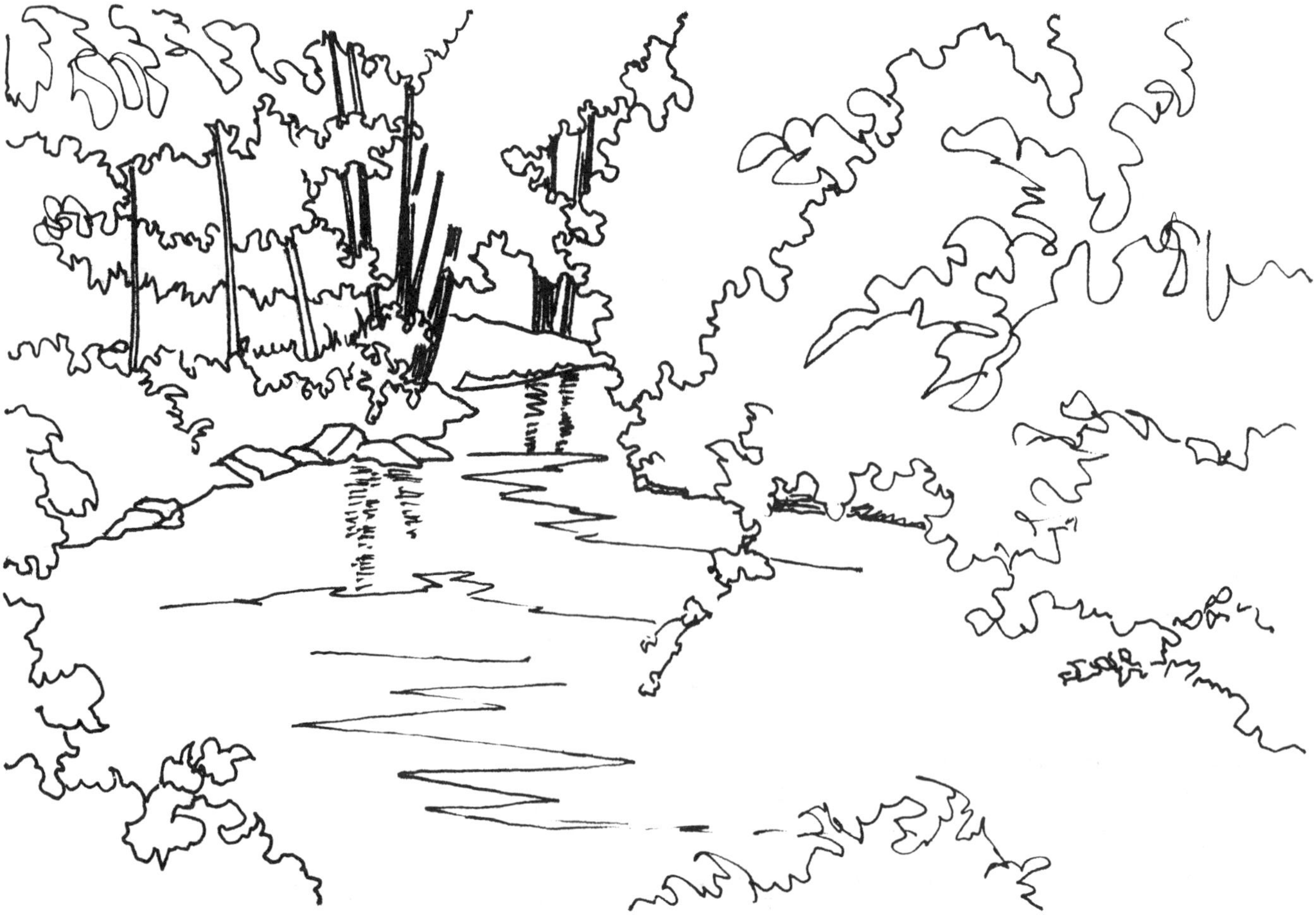

## HOUSE ON FOX ROAD

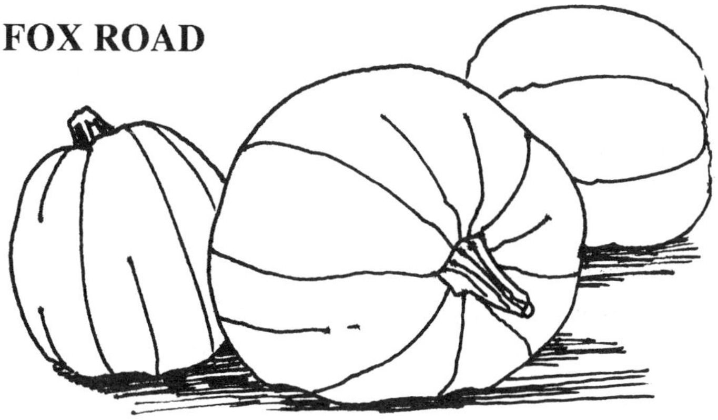

**PAPER SIZE:** 11" x 15"

**PALETTE**

Burnt Umber
Cobalt Blue
Cadmium Orange
Winsor Violet
Raw Sienna
Winsor Blue
New Gamboge
Burnt Sienna
Cadmium Red
Neutral Tint

Transfer the pattern. Mask out the snow on the branches of the small tree following directions given at the front of this book.

**SKY AND BACKGROUND TREES**

Mix the following:
Light Value Cobalt Blue
Medium Value Burnt Umber + Burnt Sienna
Dark Value Violet Gray (Winsor Violet + Brown Madder + Winsor Blue)
Dark Value Navy Blue (Winsor Blue + Brown Madder)

Using the light value Cobalt Blue and the 1 inch flat brush, wet the paper from the horizon line all the way up to the top edge. Carefully wet around the house. (You may find it easier to use the 8 round brush to wet next to the house, but switch back to the 1 inch brush to apply the paint). Check the paper to see if it is evenly shiny - that is, no puddles and no dry spots. If so, you're ready to go! Load the medium value Burnt Umber + Burnt Sienna into the brush and stroke DOWNWARD from the top of the tree line so that the trees won't float out into the sky area. So, for the same reason, pull upward from the horizon line. The background tree area should be pretty well covered with this mix, but it won't be smooth looking. You will see brush strokes as well as lighter and darker areas. Now, pick up the dark value violet gray (Winsor Violet + Brown Madder + Winsor Blue) and stroke it on in the same way, but just here and there. Carefully "draw" the color around the buildings with the tip of the 8 round brush. Now, check to see if the paper is still shiny EVERYWHERE. If it is not, stop, blow it completely dry, then rewet and continue. Lastly, pick up dark value navy blue (Winsor Blue + Brown Madder) with your brush. Use this mix to darken the tree line. It will look especially nice along the horizon as well as behind the white buildings.

You will see brush strokes with this technique and that's OK. However, if they are a bit too obvious, you can soften them. Rinse the brush, blot it, fan it a bit and ever so lightly blend with the brush half on the color and half off of it. The wetter the paper, the softer your touch. Remember too, if the paper is quite wet, the color will probably soften ON IT'S OWN. So, why not leave it alone? Let it dry.

Look at your background washes. Do you like it? Is it too light? Too Blah? You can adjust it now with drybrushing. Use any of the colors you've already used in the background. The paper should be dry for this step. Use a rake brush, or dampen the 8 round brush, then squeeze all the water out with a paper towel. Pinch the bristles at the ferrule to spread them out until your brush looks like a little fan brush. Dip it into your wash. (If it closes up, you have too much wash in it). Now, lightly drag the brush over the surface of your dry paper. This texture will add depth to your tree line. You can also add color or darken the trees if you apply 2 or 3 coats, letting them dry in between. Then pull up lots of liner trees, tucking them in and out of the dry brushing. Some should be complete trees, but not all! Don't make them all perfect! Your landscapes will look much more realistic if you paint in this way, rather than so precisely.

**BUILDINGS**

With the exception of the windows and the shadows, the buildings are actually clean, white paper. Note the clean, sharp edges of both the windows and shadows. That means that they were painted onto dry paper! Mix a medium value gray violet (you can use your gray violet tree mix + touch Winsor Violet). Using the 4 round brush carefully paint on all of the shadows under the roof lines as well as the right sides of the buildings as you see in the photo. The important thing to remember about shadows is that they have no lines. So, once you set your brush down and begin to paint - don't stop! Keep the wash moving so that a dry line won't form. When that is dry, lightly wash in the left portion of the roof with light value Cobalt Blue. Note that there's a line of dry, white paper that separates the roof from the shading there.

The windows are filled in with dark value navy blue (Winsor Blue + Brown Madder). While they're still wet, blot one corner with a kleenex. Then, use the gray violet shadow color to carefully draw around the outside of the window casing. Oops! Did you make a boo-boo? Simply use your scratch knife blade to pick out any unwanted color and even out your window lines.

**FOREGROUND GRASSY AREAS**

Mix: Light Value Raw Sienna

Medium Value Burnt Umber + Burnt Sienna

There are two small areas that will be painted with these washes - just below the tree line, one to each side of the road. Pick up a bit of the light value Raw Sienna in the tip of the 8 round brush. Begin painting the top of the grassy area just below the tree line. Move your brush back and forth horizontaly leaving small areas of clean, white paper where there are patches of snow. About half way down, pick up the medium value Burnt Umber + Burnt Sienna and finish out the grassy area. This is the base for the grass. Let this dry completely.

Now, let's paint a little grass on top of the base color. Use either a rake brush, or fan out your 8 round brush (follow the instructons under "Drybrushing" at the front of this book). Using the medium value Burnt Umber + Burnt Sienna, pull up some grasses. Do the same down the center of the road. Watch the perspective here! Note how you can barely see any grass at all near the top of the road, but it gets thicker and darker as it comes toward you. If you prefer to use a liner brush to paint these grasses, that's fine.

**GRASS IN BOTTOM LEFT CORNER**

Mix a dark value Burnt Umber and also use your dark value navy blue (Winsor Blue + Brown Madder). Prewet the entire left corner with clean water. Be sure to wet up at least an inch farther than the top of the grass to be sure to leave plenty of room for that top edge of color to soften. Otherwise, your grass will look chopped off! Check for the shine, then use the 1 inch flat brush to lay on the dark value Burnt Umber. While still wet stroke a bit of the navy blue on top of that. This should be quite dark at this point. You're going to scrape out the grasses with the handle of your 1 inch brush. But you have to be patient and wait for just the right time to do it - when the paper is just about to lose the shine. Don't worry, you'll be able to tell! Tilt the handle of the 1 inch brush slightly so that you're using a bit of the side, not the very tip. Then use a slow, steady movement to scrape out some of the paint. That, in fact, is what you are doing. You are scraping out the grasses. This is a great, fun way to do grass! Be sure that they curve gracefully and are different widths and lengths. Wait until this is dry, then add liner grass of the same colors to really make this spot look nice.

**LARGE TREES**

Mix a dark value Neutral Tint. Then base in the large tree with the medium value Burnt Umber + Burnt Sienna used in the background trees. Look for the shine. Wiggle your brush back over this wash to be sure that the entire tree is evenly shiny. Now, pick up a bit of the dark value Neutral Tint in the tip of the 8 round brush. Dab this onto the right side of the tree, letting it float outward if it wishes. Now, quickly while it's still wet, pick up a stylus or a very sharp pencil and "draw" on the bark. Yes, that's right! Simply draw a lot of horizontal lines all over the tree. Easy, huh? Of course, you are not actually drawing lines at all. What happens is you dent the paper with the sharp object and the paint runs into the dent. Let it dry, then take a look. If it still seems rather plain, do a few liner strokes over it. Or, is it too dark? Try just a few liner strokes with white acrylic or gesso.

The main trunk of the small tree is painted in the same way. Then paint on all of the little branches and limbs with Neutral Tint on your liner brush. When it's totally dry, erase the masking fluid from the snow on it's branches. Shade the bottom of that snow by floating on a bit of medium value navy blue (Winsor Blue + Brown Madder).

**PUMPKINS**

Mix the following:
Light Value New Gamboge
Medium Value Orange (Cadmium Orange + Cadmium Red)
Medium Value Rust (Brown Madder + Burnt Sienna)

Take a look at the two pumpkins and note that the right one is much lighter than the other. That's what separates the two. Keeping that in mind, use the 4 round brush to base the front one with light value New Gamboge. Try leaving a couple of tiny lines of dry, white paper to separate the "sections" of the pumpkins. It helps give them form. While the New Gamboge is still wet, touch a tiny bit of medium value orange along the bottom. Let it just float out however it wishes. Don't blend it to death! After it's dry, base the back pumpkin with light value New Gamboge, then touch a bit of orange mix at the top and the rust mix along the bottom. Try to get the color nice and dark where it goes behind the other pumpkin. When the pumpkins are dry, paint on little stems of Burnt Umber, or even Neutral Tint if you want them darker.

**SHADOWS**

Mix medium value navy blue (Winsor Blue + Brown Madder) for your shadow color. Be sure that this is a color that you like! Is it gray enough, or do you prefer it more blue? Adjust it by adding or subtracting Winsor Blue.

Now, remember what we said earlier about shadows. They can be soft edged or hard edged, but they have no lines! So, take a moment to plan your attack before you actually start to paint. Break it up into as many small sections as you can, because once you set your brush down you must keep it moving until you finish that area. For small areas (such as along the edge of the grassy area, or under the pumpkins) use the tip of the 8 round brush. However, use the 1 inch brush for the large shadowy area across the bottom of the painting. Be sure you have a large amount of the mix ready, then load the brush fully and take off. Work on dry paper and simply keep moving the brush before the wash has a chance to lose the shine. If you mess up and put some where it doesn't go - keep going. Pretend like you meant to do it all along, and everyone else will think you did too!

**Matting Suggestions** - Outside, Crescent 3297 Inside, Crescent 977

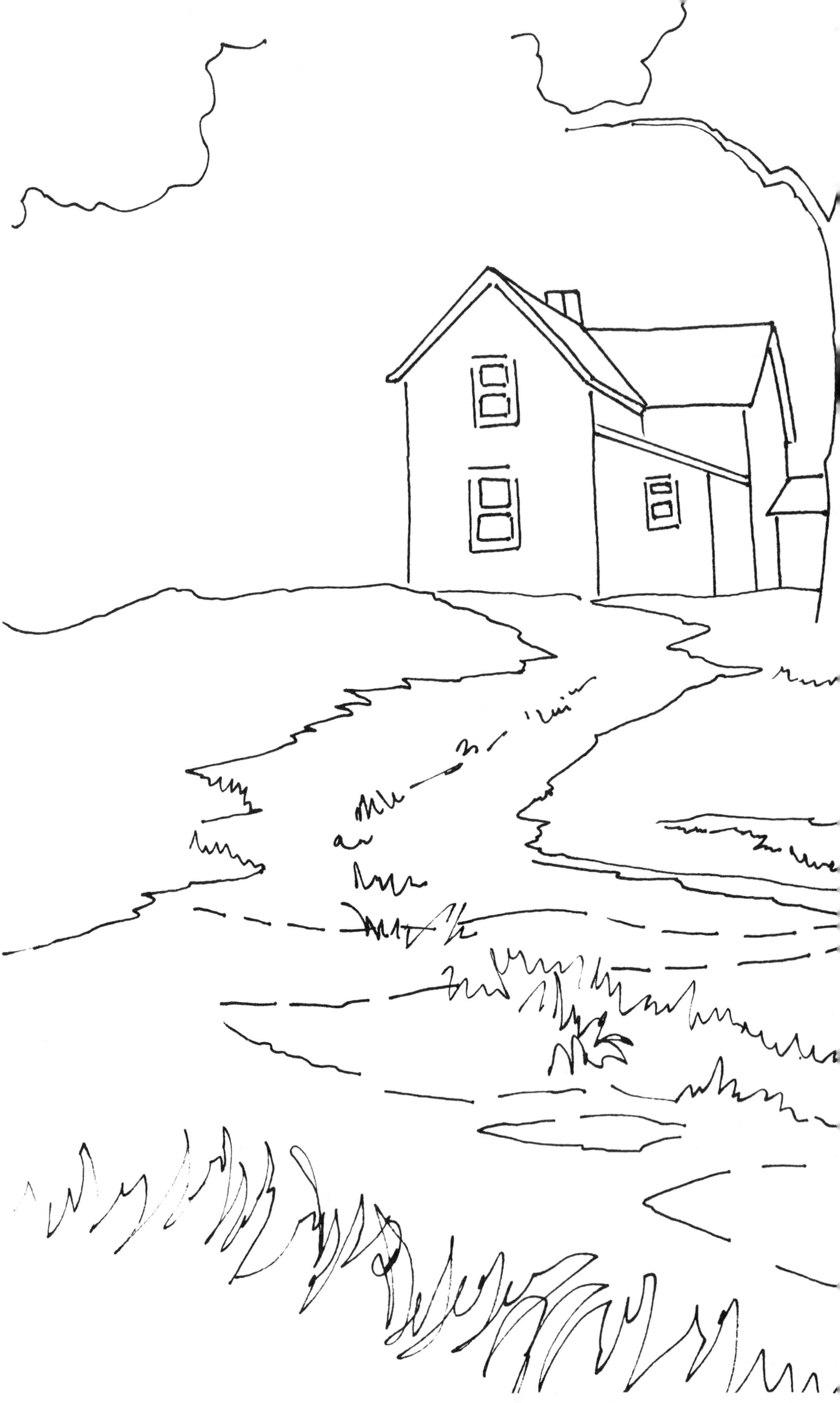

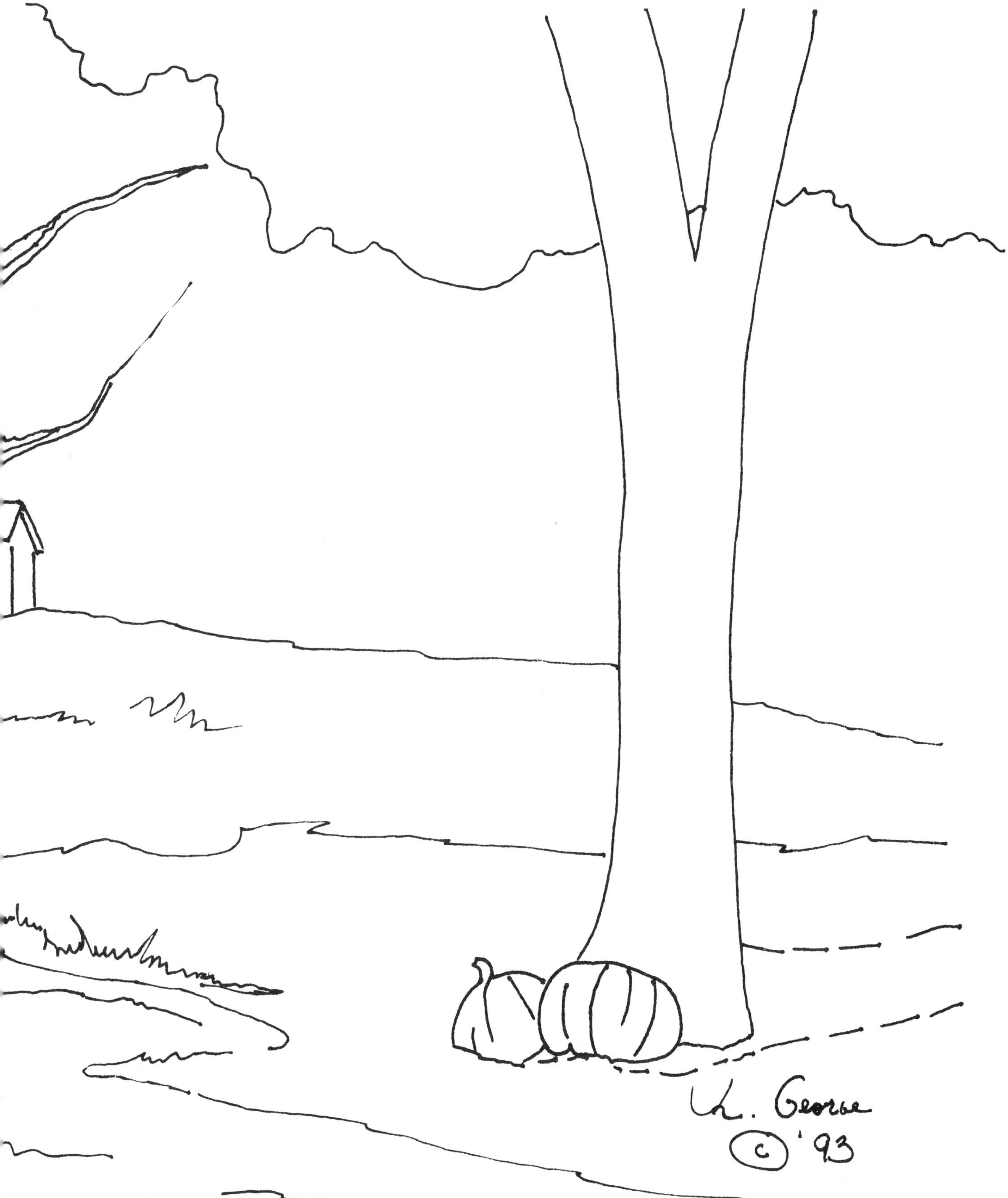


HOUSE ON FOX ROAD

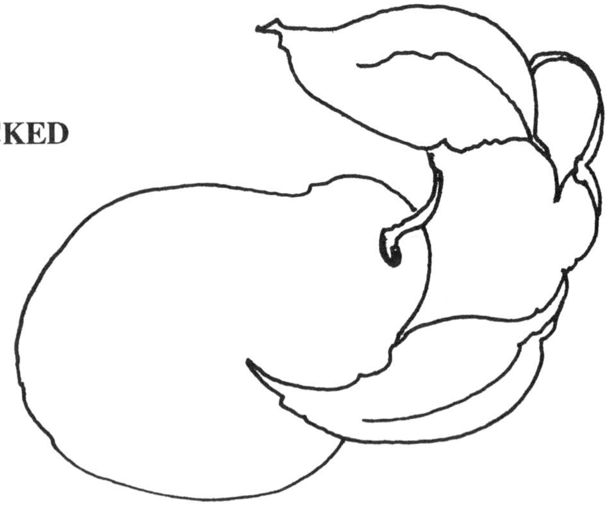

# JUST PICKED

**PAPER SIZE:** 11 " X 15"

**PALETTE**

New Gamboge
Winsor Blue
Brown Madder
Alizarin Crimson
Viridian
Burnt Sienna
Burnt Umber
Ultramarine Blue
Cobalt Blue

Transfer the pattern following the directions at the front of this book.

These pears have just been picked off of my sister's tree. She lives on a farm and has many fruit trees. The fruit isn't always picture perfect...they have a personality all their own.

## DARK SECTION OF WINDOW

Let's begin by painting the darker sections of the window that you see at the top, right corner. Mix a medium value grayed violet (Ultramarine Blue + Alizarin Crimson + touch of Burnt Umber). This color actually butts right up against the white wooden parts of the window. See it? Begin painting there, right next to where the window frame will be white, and fill in that entire dark corner with this gray violet. Remember, when you fill in an area DON'T OUTLINE! or that outline will dry and always be a little darker than the rest. So, start at one side and fill as you go. While this area is drying mix a dark value navy blue (Winsor Blue + Brown Madder).

When everything is totally dry, darken that upper most section only, with the dark value navy blue mixture. Once again, let it dry thoroughly. Now, pull a bit of the dark value navy blue mix out to the side and add water until it is a light value. On your pattern, locate a dotted line inside the areas you've just finished painting. Got it? Now, look at the photo to see that just to the left of that line the violet is a bit darker. So, use the lightened navy blue mix to wash over the violet section to the left of that dotted line. While this is drying mix: Shadow on the Window:

Medium Value Blue (Winsor Blue + Brown Madder + Cobalt Blue)
Medium Value Violet (Alizarin Crimson + Ultramarine Blue)
NOTE: Burnt Umber is not used to mix this violet, therefore it is not grayed.

This may seem a bit strange, doing the shadow first. There is a good reason, though. There are a lot of cracks and peeling paint on this old window, and they would smudge when the shadow was painted over them. So, let's do the shadow first!

This shadow is also indicated by a dotted line on the pattern. Use the 1 inch brush and load it well with the medium value blue mix (Winsor Blue + Brown Madder + Cobalt Blue). The shadow falls only over the white sections of the window, so there is no need to paint it onto that dark corner section. Set the brush down at the top of the page and brush back and forth, gradually moving downward and filling in as you go. Don't go any further to the left than the dotted line. When you have the shadow area completely filled in, rinse the brush and pick up a bit of the medium value violet (Ultramarine Blue + Alizarin Crimson) and dab it onto the still shiny shadow. Just a bit at the base of the window will do. Remember, don't go back into the shadow for any reason once the paper has lost it's shine!! This is very important. Shadows are smooth and leave no lines. Once the paper has lost the shine, each time you touch the brush to the paper it will pick up paint and make a mark. So, put that paint on there, relax and leave it alone!!

## SEPARATING THE SECTIONS

Separate each piece of moulding by shading with medium value navy blue (Winsor Blue + Brown Madder). Let's take it a section at a time. Looking at the right side of the window frame, there are several vertical sections. Begin with the first section. It's the largest one. Wet it completely with clean, clear water. Look for a nice, even shine. Then, using the 8 round brush, pick up a bit of the medium value navy blue (Winsor Blue + Brown Madder) and dab all down the left side of the wet section - right up next to the dry, white paper. Use a "dabbing" motion, and each time you lift the brush a little puff of water will start the navy blue spreading outward. Quickly, rinse the brush, blot it, fan it out a bit and soften the color out to the right. So, this shading color should be darkest on the left and soften out gradually to the right. Let this dry thoroughly.

The next piece of moulding will be painted differently. Put your finger on the left edge of the section you just finished painting. Now, move it over TWO vertical lines. That will be the left edge of the new piece of moulding. This piece is divided by a vertical line down the center, right? The right half will not be painted. This time, wet to the left of that center vertical line. Using the 4 round brush, pick up the medium value navy blue (Winsor Blue + Brown Madder) and dab it onto the RIGHT side of the wet area, right up next to the clean, dry paper. Once again, rinse the brush, blot it and fan it out. Then gently catch the outside edge of color and fade it out to the LEFT. So, this time the color is darkest on the right and is softened out to the left. Let this dry.

On to the next section. This one is easy. Simply fill in the entire section with medium value navy blue (Winsor Blue + Brown Madder) and let it dry.

Move over one vertical line. This large section is not painted. However, the next small section to the left will be. Wet that entire small section and dab the medium value navy blue onto it's RIGHT side. Also put on a dab or two of the medium value violet (Ultramarine Blue + Alizarin Crimson). Rinse the brush and soften the color out to the LEFT. After it has dried, wet the final vertical section with clean water. Float the medium value navy blue mix onto the right side and fade it out to the left as before.

Now for the horizontal sections. Start with those tiny horizontal sections right at the top. There are three of them and they are all painted the same way. Wet them, one at a time, and float the medium value navy blue (Winsor Blue + Brown Madder) at the bottom edge. Set the 4 round brush down at the right side first because the color is darkest there. Then, slowly drag it across to the left. It should get a bit lighter as you go. Don't be afraid to add a bit of extra color at the right, if necessary.

Directly under those small sections you have just painted is the large one. Just under it is where the window would open. There should be a dark crack there. Use the liner brush and dark value navy blue (Winsor Blue + Brown Madder). Paint it onto dry paper!

Lastly, the large remaining section should be shaded along the front edge. Use the 8 round brush to float medium value navy blue to the left of the pears. Quickly, rinse the brush and with a bit of clean water, soften the top edge of the blue. While this is all drying, mix:

## CRACKS AND PEELING PAINT

There are two mixes of crack colors because the color changes depending on whether the cracks are in shade or sun. They are all painted onto dry paper. Simply fill them in with the correct color. Note that cracks are also darker in the shade, and look much lighter in bright sun.

Shade - Medium Value Blue Gray (Ultramarine Blue + Burnt Umber)

Sun - Medium Value Brown Gray (Ultramarine Blue + Burnt Umber + Burnt Sienna)

Areas where the paint has peeled are painted the same way and with the same colors, with one exception. After those areas have dried, draw along the top edge with a fine line of the same color. Look at the area just to the left of the pears. There you can see a large area of peeling paint. See the dark line work just under the clean, white paper? That's what makes it look as though the paint is raised slightly. Easy, but effective!

**WALL**

Fill in that entire dark wall section (that's the vertical section on the extreme right side of the page) with a dark value gray (Ultramarine Blue + Burnt Umber). If it seems rather "dead" afterward, try glazing over it with medium value Burnt Sienna. That should perk it up!

**PEARS**

These pears have just been picked and are sitting on the sill to ripen a bit. The painting technique for all of the pears is the same, but the color changes. Not because they actually were a different color, rather for the sake of the painting. All of them should not be equally "pretty" or bright. Those that are off to one side, or in the background, should not capture your attention as much as those in the center of interest. That, after all, is what helps you to develop a center of interest.

Keep that in mind as you mix the following colors:

Medium Value Yellow Green (Viridian + New Gamboge+ Burnt Sienna)
Dark Value Green (Winsor Blue + New Gamboge + Burnt Umber)
Medium Value Rust (Burnt Umber + Burnt Sienna + Brown Madder)
Medium Value Raw Sienna

Begin with those two rather ugly pears on the right side. You may practice on those. Wet them down, one at a time with clean water. Float a bit of the medium value yellow green onto the very top, then pick up the dark value green (Winsor Blue + New Gamboge + Burnt Umber) and dab onto the bottom half of the pear. Allow the dark to spread upward some. Soften any hard edges of color. Remember, these two should remain very dull in comparison with the other pears. When they've lost the shine, pick up one tiny drop of the rust mix (Burnt Umber + Burnt Sienna + Brown Madder) in the tip of the liner brush. Touch it to the slightly damp surface. These spots should soften slightly, but still hold their shape.

Now, for the other three. Wet the center pear with medium value Raw Sienna. While the color is still wet and shiny, dab a bit of the medium value yellow green (Viridian + New Gamboge + Burnt Sienna) at the back. Rinse the brush, fan it and soften any hard edges. Now, check for a shine. If it's still there, dab a bit of rust onto the front, near the bottom. Once again, rinse the brush and soften hard edges. (If the pear wasn't shiny, dry it completely, then rewet with clean water and then dab on the rust)!

The remaining pears have a little more detail. Wet one with light value Raw Sienna and be sure it is evenly shiny. Then, pick up medium value yellow green (Viridian + New Gamboge + Burnt Sienna) in the 8 round brush and stroke on the color. Use a stroke that "contours" the fruit. That is, follow the shape of the pear. It's round, so draw on the color as if you were actually touching the outside of the pear with your brush. Use quite a bit of this yellow green. Rinse the brush and soften hard edges. Each of these two pears have a highlighted area that remains lighter than the rest. Try to keep the greens out of this area. If color floats over it, simply squeeze all of the water out of the brush and wipe back the color using pressure. After the yellow green is on and blended, blow it dry. Then, rewet with clean water and stroke on a little dark value green (Winsor Blue + New Gamboge + Burnt Umber) to shade the pears. On the left pear, the dark green goes along the bottom. For the other, place the dark green at the back and along the bottom. Sometimes it takes three or four times to really get the pear as dark as you want it to be. That's O.K.! I do that, too! Just be sure to let it dry thoroughly in between, and use very clean water to rewet. You may also use a bit of the medium value rust (Burnt Umber + Burnt Sienna + Brown Madder), if you wish.

## FOREGROUND

After the pears have dried, base in the entire foreground with a light value brown (Burnt Umber + Burnt Sienna). When it has dried, paint on the shadows. The color mixes you will use are:

Medium Value Gray Violet (Ultramarine Blue + Alizarin Crimson + touch Burnt Umber)

Medium Value Navy (Winsor Blue + Brown Madder)

Beginning at the right, just under the "ugly" pears, paint in that entire shadow with the gray violet mix. While it is still wet and shiny, dab on the medium value navy blue under the "uglies" to darken the shadow there.

Moving across to the left, paint the shadow under the two remaining pears. Once again, begin with the medium value gray violet in front, and as you paint around to the side pick up medium value navy to finish up and darken.

The dark shadow all along the bottom of the page is painted in two coats. First, the medium value gray violet (Ultramarine Blue + Alizarin Crimson + touch Burnt Umber). Let it dry thoroughly, then glaze over with medium value navy (Winsor Blue + Brown Madder).

Finally, spatter the foreground to simulate a concrete or stone surface. You might wish to cover the pears and window if you've never spattered before! Use the shadow colors for the spatter. There are some great tips on spattering at the front of this book. There, all done! You could use this idea with any kind of fruit...or maybe even put a curtain in the window!

**Matting Suggestions:** Outside - Crescent 33, Inside - Crescent 995

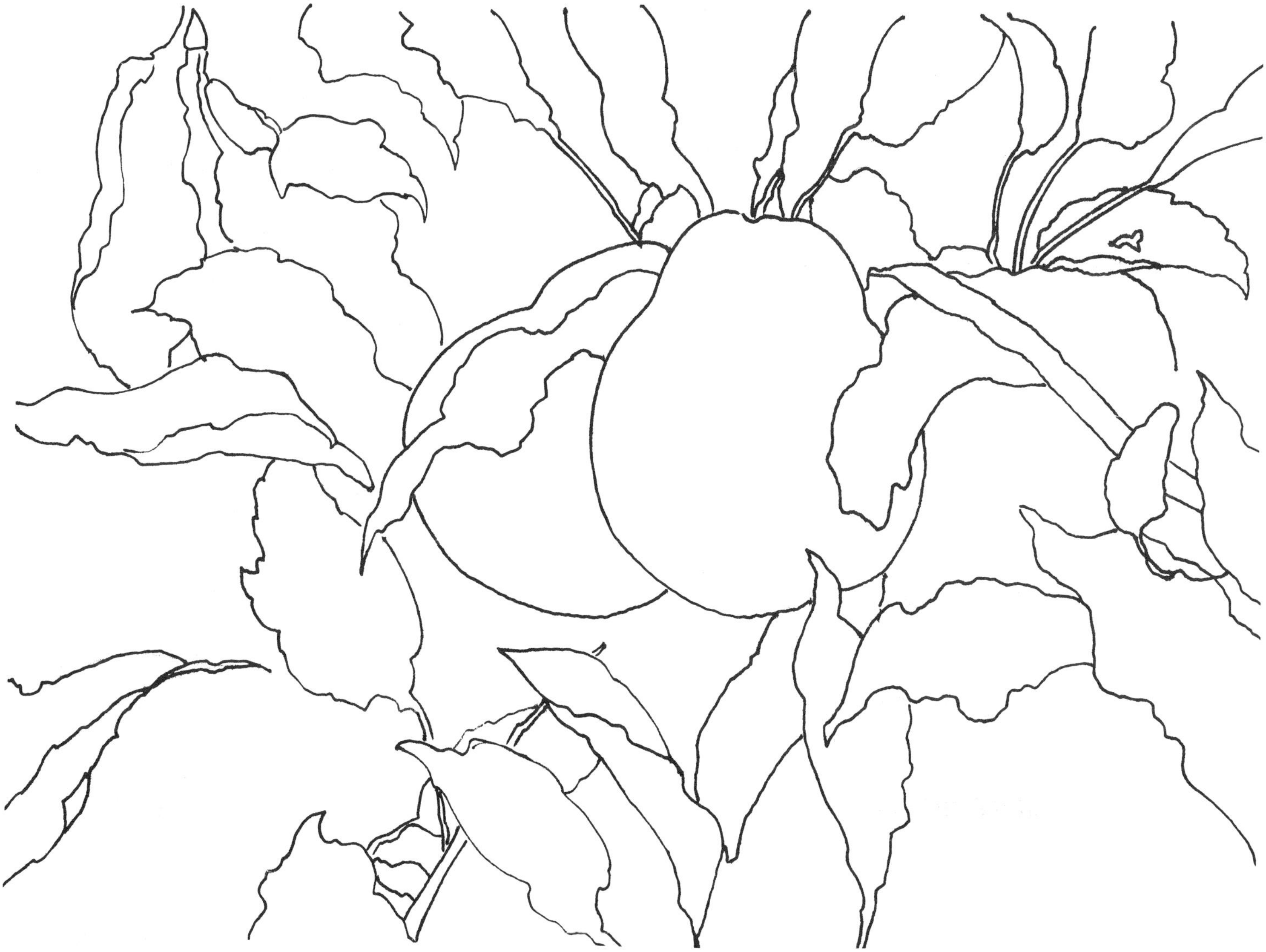

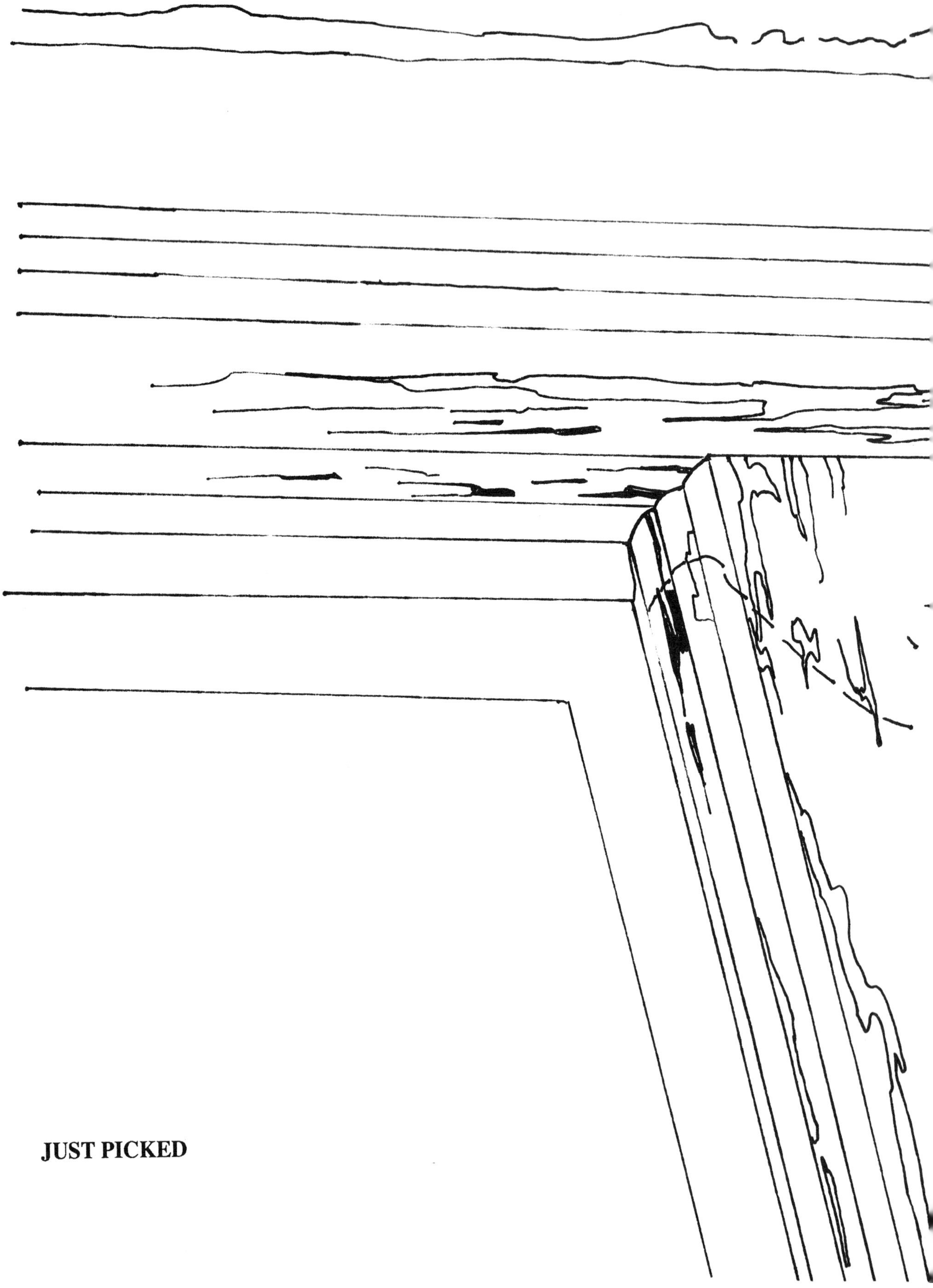

JUST PICKED

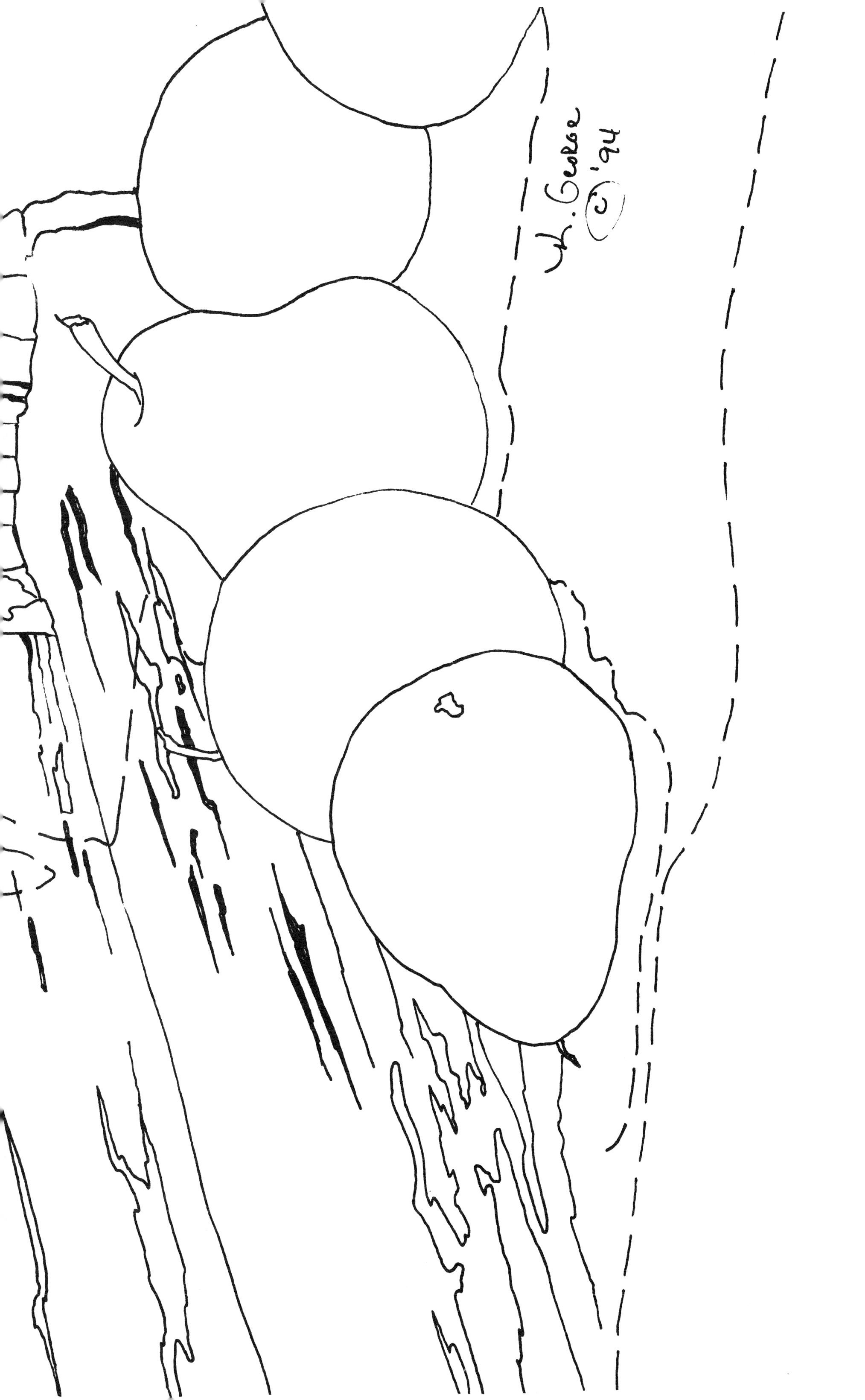
H. George ©'94

## SUNNY POPPIES

**PAPER SIZE:** 9-1/2" x 12"

**PALETTE**

Winsor Blue
Alizarin Crimson
Ultramarine Blue
Cadmium Orange
Burnt Sienna
New Gamboge
Brown Madder
Burnt Umber

Transfer the pattern following the directions at the front of this book. Keep all of your pencil lines within the white flowers very light. However, be sure that you see all of the leaves and stems clearly. You will be painting over them, so the pencil line has to hold.

This particular painting has a lot of "negative" painting. If you've never done negative painting before, this is a good one to start out on.

**BACKGROUND**

Mix the following:

Medium Value Pink (Alizarin Crimson + Burnt Sienna)

Medium Value Blue (Ultramarine Blue + touch of Burnt Sienna)

Wet the entire paper. Use a large brush and look for a nice, EVEN shine! No puddles, and no dry spots. Pick up a bit of the pink mix to the 1" brush and LAY ON the color here and there. Don't be afraid to let some of this color spread onto the flower petals, but TRY NOT TO LOSE ALL OF THE WHITE! Now, take a look at the paper. Is it still evenly wet and shiny? (If not, the best thing to do is stop, blow it dry, rewet and continue). Pick up some of the blue mix in the 1" brush and place it here and there, again mostly staying away from the petals. I know, this is scary, so here are some rules: yes, the blue can go over the pink areas; it can even go onto the petals, but all background colors should be very soft, no hard edges. At this point, your background will not look anything like the finished painting, you background will be much lighter. Remember, this is just a background...it's what you do on top of it that makes the painting. No matter what your background looks like, you can follow the same steps and have a wonderful painting! So, relax!!

Let the paper dry completely.

**CENTERS**

Do the center next. It will add some pizazz to the painting, as well as give you a "feeling" for the poppies.

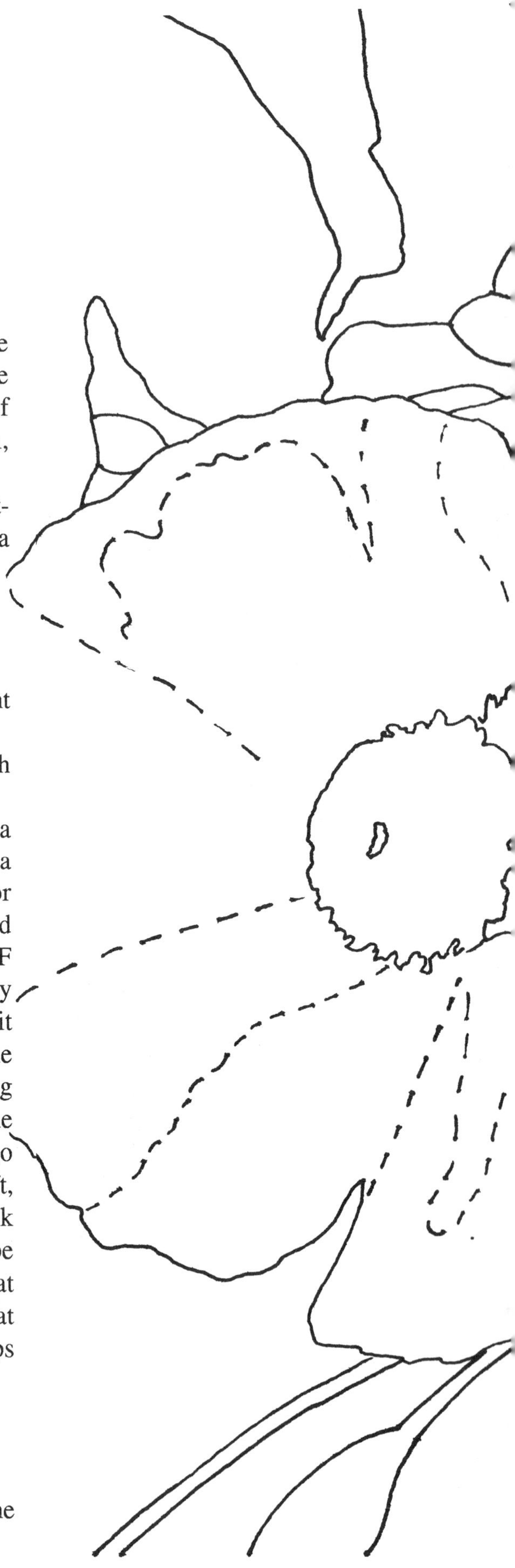

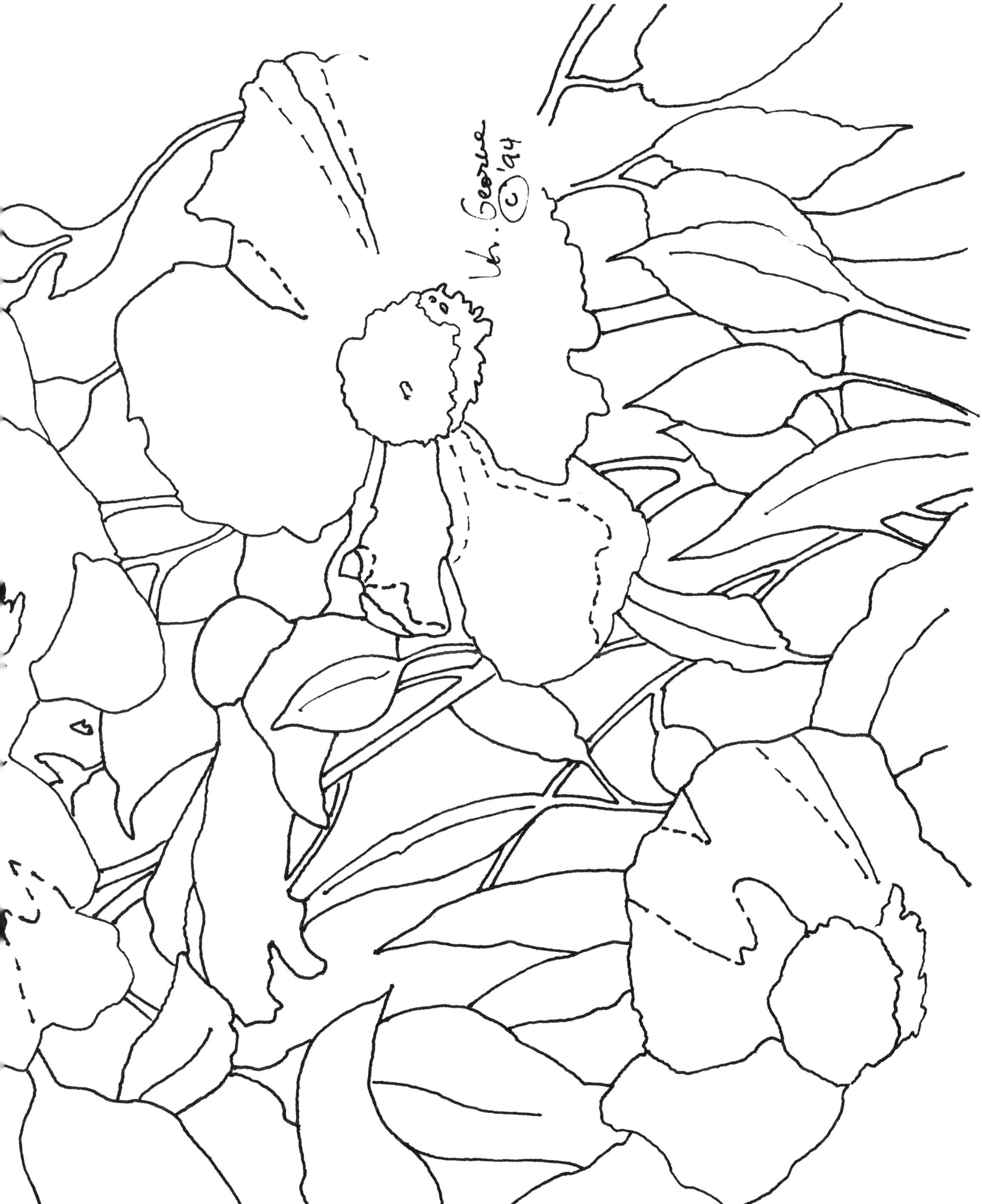

Painting one at a time, base a center with light value New Gamboge. While the New Gamboge is still wet, pick up a bit of medium value Burnt Sienna in the tip of the 4 round brush and lightly tap it onto the entire front of the center. Because the background is wet, the Burnt Sienna should soften slightly. Don't be surprised if it softens too much and seems too light. (That happens to me all of the time)! Simply let it dry, rewet it, and dab on more Burnt Sienna. Note that the poppy center at the bottom of the page, as well as the one in the background have less detail than the others.

**LEAVES AND STEMS**

Painting one at a time, base a center with light value New Gamboge. While the New Gamboge is still wet, pick up a bit of medium value Burnt Sienna in the tip of the 4 round brush and lightly tap it onto the entire front of the center. Because the background is wet, the Burnt Sienna should soften slightly. Don't be surprised if it softens too much and seems too light. (That happens to me all of the time)! Simply let it dry, rewet it, and dab on more Burnt Sienna. Note that the poppy center at the bottom of the page, as well as the one in the background have less detail than the others.

**LEAVES AND STEMS**

All of the leaves, stems and one poppy are painted "negatively". This simply means that instead of directly painting all of those things, you paint the background AROUND THEM a bit darker. Suddenly, they appear! This is great fun, and once you understand how to do it, it will add so much to your watercolors!!

Mix these colors:

Light Value Blue (Ultramarine Blue + touch Burnt Sienna)
A Medium Value of the Same
Medium Value Navy Blue (Winsor Blue + Brown Madder)
Medium Value Blue Green (Winsor Blue + Burnt Umber)

Before you begin to paint, take a good look at the photo. See that the top right of the background looks much darker than the middle or the bottom sections? Keep this in mind as you begin to paint. Ready? Think of the background now as sort of jigsaw puzzle. The flowers are pieces, the leaves are pieces, and the spaces BETWEEN the leaves and flowers are also pieces. It's these in-between spaces that you'll be painting. That's negative painting! I suggest that you start with your lightest value (light value blue - Ultramarine Blue + Burnt Sienna). Begin to fill in between some of the leaves with this color. The sections between the leaves are so small there's really no need to prewet the paper. So, just work on it dry. (Remember, don't outline the area before you fill it in, because that outline will dry and leave the outline darker). Soon you will see them begin to appear.

When you've painted quite a sew sections and are feeling more confident, begin to darken those at the top right and along the left side of the painting. At the top darken sections with medium value navy blue (Winsor Blue + Brown Madder). Along the left side, darken with medium value blue (Ultramarine Blue + Burnt Sienna) or touches of medium value green (Winsor Blue + Burnt Umber). Remember now, those sections get pretty light by the time they reach the center of the painting. This must be done gradually, not all at once. After all, you want it to seem as through the background was painted in one step, not be obvious that you painted around all of the leaves! To paint a section that goes from a dark value to a light one, prewet it first with clean water. Then dab a bit of the dark color onto one side, rinse the brush, and lightly soften out any hard edges of color. (See the front of this book for more detailed instructions on blending).

All that's left now is to paint a bit of color onto a few of the leaves. Pick a few and give them a simple vein line. To do that, wet one side of the leaf with the 4 round brush. Pick up one drop of medium value green (Winsor Blue + Burnt Umber) in the tip of the brush and dab it onto the wet side,

**WHITE POPPIES**

These are the shading colors for the flower petals:

Light Value Cadmium Orange

Medium Value Purple (Ultramarine Blue + Alizarin Crimson +touch of Brown Madder)

Try to keep the shadows on the white petals as fresh and clean as possible. How do you accomplish that? There's only one way - lay that color on there, and don't play with it! Trust me on this. Lay the color on and leave it alone and you will like it much more than if you smooshed it to death.

All of the shadow areas are marked for you with dotted lines on your pattern. The majority of the shading is painted with the purple mix. Pick up just a drop in the tip of the 8 round brush. Occasionally, a shadow lightens from medium value to light value. Set your brush down where the color is the darkest, then rinse the brush, pick up a drop of clean water and continue painting, dragging the color out lighter and lighter.

Another type of shadow you can try is a two-color shadow. If you look at the bottom half of the largest poppy, you'll see that type of shadow. To paint it, pick up the purple mix (Ultramarine Blue + Alizarin Crimson + touch Brown Madder) in the 8 round brush and lay it onto the darkest section of shadow. Quickly, rinse the brush and pick up a drop of light value Cadmium Orange. Start painting with the orange right where you left off with the purple mix. Actually touch the orange to the wet edge of the purple so that they begin to mix - but DON'T MIX THEM YOURSELF! Let them do what they want. Just stand back and watch how beautiful it looks, and take credit for it! Please remember, half of the secret to watercolor is to not work so hard! Relax, and let paint and water do the work. If you can do that, your painting will be oh so fresh, clean and wonderful!!!!

**Matting Suggestions** - Outer Crescent 3301, Inner Crescent 1503

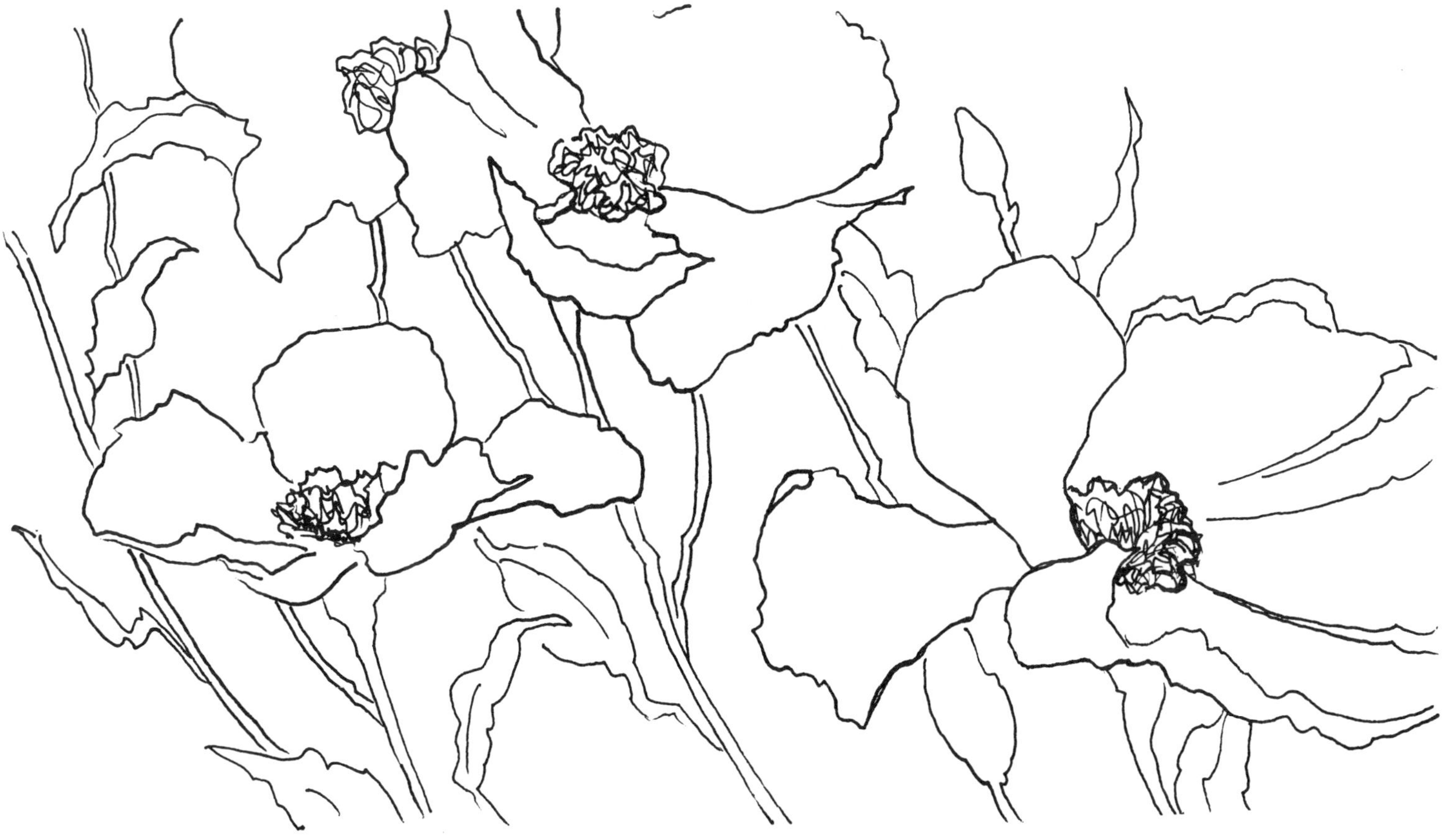

## SOME FAVORITE THINGS

**PAPER SIZE:** 8" x 15"

**PALETTE**

Winsor Blue
Winsor Red
Cadmium Orange
Cobalt Blue
Burnt Umber
Brown Madder
Alizarin Crimson
New Gamboge
Winsor Violet
Neutral Tint

This is a still life that I actually set up myself. After it was set up outside, I took several photos of it from different directions. Taking photos is a great way to begin painting your own subjects. You can enlarge the photo on a copy machine and take a pattern off of it. If the photo is too dark to enlarge, try placing a piece of tracing paper on top of the original photo. Trace from the photo, then enlarge the pattern from the tracing paper!

Transfer the pattern following the directions at the front of this book.

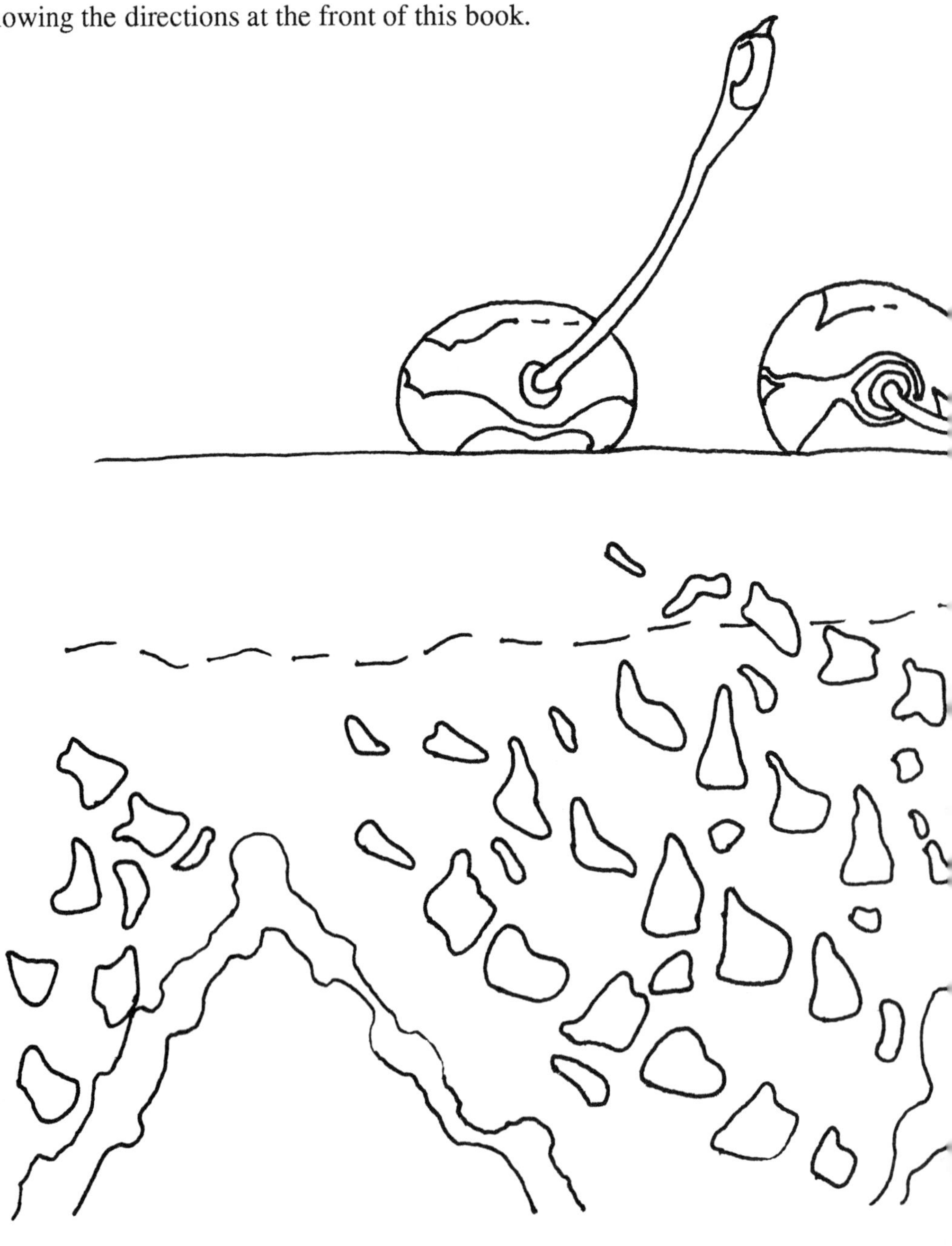

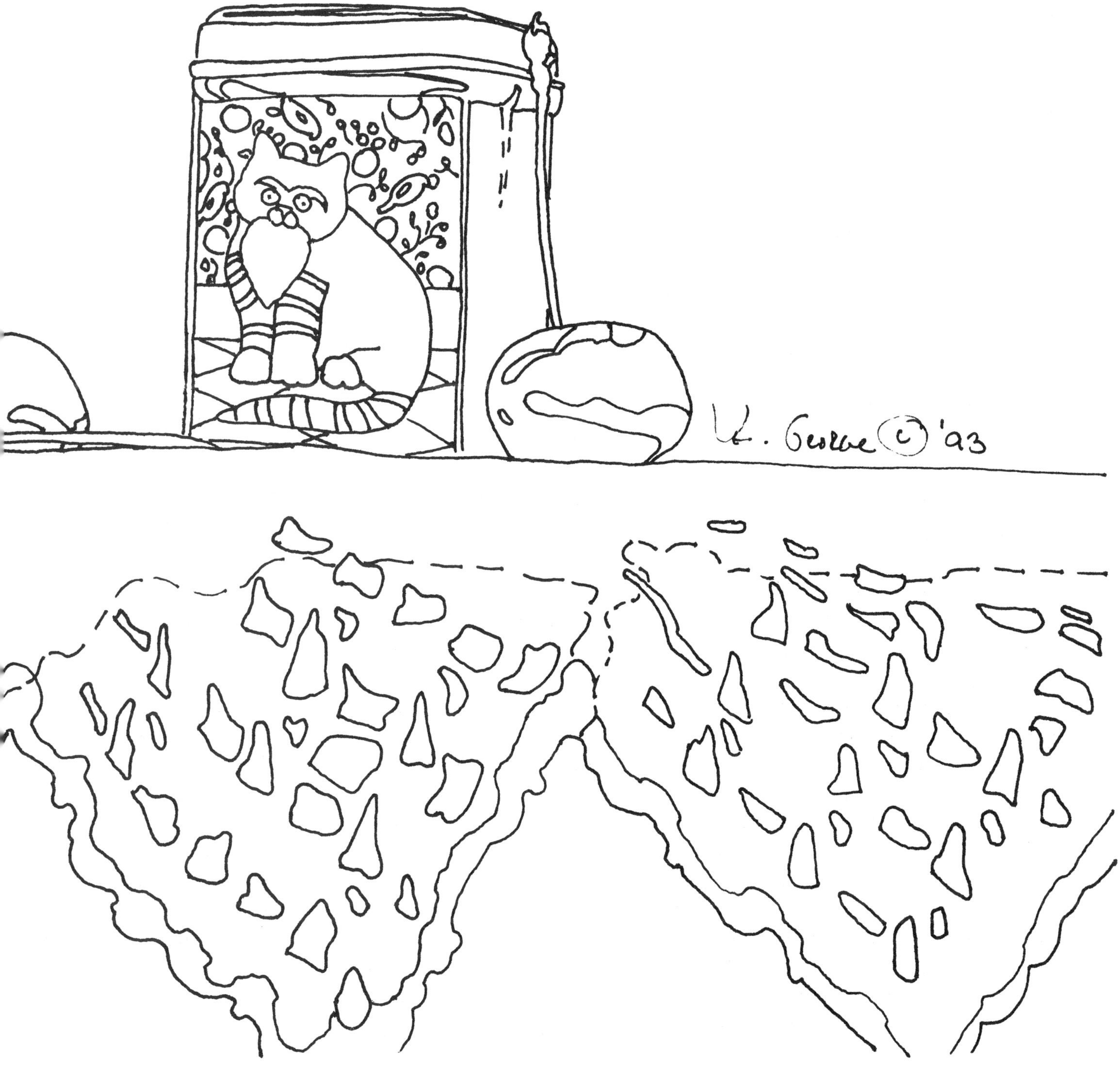
K. George © '93

## BACKGROUND

Mix a large puddle of medium value Cobalt Blue. Set this aside and wet the background, from the table to the top of the paper, with clean water. Use the 8 round brush to carefully wet around the cherries and the tin, but switch to the 1 inch brush to finish. Be sure to check for a nice, even SHINE...no puddles and no dry spots! Then pick up the medium value Cobalt Blue on the 1 inch brush and stroke it onto the right side of the painting. Drag it to the left, allowing the color to lighten as it goes. By the time you reach the left side of the paper, the paper should be completely white. Use the 8 round brush to carefully "push" the Cobalt Blue right up to the edge of the cherries and the tin. Keep an eye on the paper. Once it loses the shine, don't go back and mess. Remember that once the shine is gone, each time the brush touches the paper it picks up paint and makes a streak! So, leave it alone. If the background is not dark enough, let it dry completely, rewet it and then apply more paint. Let this dry completely.

## TIN

Mix a medium value Cadmium Orange and base in the background behind the cat. Also, base in the entire right side of the tin and the little tile squares under the kitty. While this is drying mix the following colors:

Medium Value Red-Orange (Cadmium Red + Cadmium Orange)
Medium Value Cadmium Red
Medium Value Red (Alizarin Crimson + touch Cadmium Red)

**Lid** - Begin with the lid. There are several "layers" to the lid, so you may find that you have to refer to your pattern or photo for assistance here. Look at the very tip top of the lid. See the tiny line of red surrounded by white highlights on both sides? Paint that in - pick up medium value red-orange (Cadmium Red + Cadmium Orange) in your liner brush. Begin painting on the right side because that side should be darkest and get lighter as you move to the left. If the color doesn't lighten just blot it with a finger or paper towel. After this has dried, paint the main section of the lid using the same color mix and the 4 round brush. Set the brush down onto the left side and fill in this entire section. Then, quickly while the color is still damp, rinse the brush and blot it out completely. Use a pressure stroke to wipe out two vertical highlights at the corner. Just keep wiping until the highlight begins to appear.

There is a silver metal section all along the bottom of the lid. Begin by painting a dark shadow line just catching the bottom edge of the red main section. (Use dark value navy blue - Winsor Blue + Brown Madder). Leave a thin line of dry, white paper then paint another dark shadow line of dark value navy blue under it. Let this all dry thoroughly. Pull a bit of the navy blue mix out to the side and water until it is a light value. Carefully, wash it over the line of white paper - except for the extreme left edge. That should remain a nice, white highlight. Once again, let this dry, then move down and paint the next section.

Base in this next little section with a light value Cadmium Red. When it's dry, use medium value red (Alizarin Crimson + touch Cadmium Red) and the 4 round brush to fill in all but the light area across the front. Just paint it onto dry paper, there's no blending. Use the same color and your liner brush to paint a tiny stripe drown the left side of the tin...then all of the stripes on the right side. Don't worry about those stripes. They don't have to be perfect - mine certainly aren't! As a last resort, just fill in the entire right side with the red mix. Behind the Cat - Fill in the little background shapes on dry paper. Just use whichever brush you feel comfortable with. The circle shapes are medium value Cadmium Red. Look carefully, are those little bird shapes? Yes! Paint those with medium value brown (Burnt Umber + a touch Winsor Violet). Finally, mix a bit of medium value green (New Gamboge + Winsor Blue + Burnt Umber) for the tiny leaves. When dry, paint the dark band of color below with dark value gray brown (Burnt Umber + Neutral Tint).

The red tiles are medium value Alizarin Crimson + Brown Madder.

## CAT

The white areas of the cat are clean, white paper. Mix a dark value Neutral Tint for the rest of him. Just fill him in, working on dry paper, painting around all of his white places. When dry, dampen the 4 round brush and use a "pressure" stroke to lift a bit of color from the right side of his head. Now his head will be a bit lighter than this back, and this is what will separate them. Shade his little white feet by carefully wetting them with clean water and touching a bit of the Neutral Tint at their tops. Quickly rinse the brush and soften the color downward. Shade his chest the same way.

His eyes are green. Use the green that you already have mixed on your palette (medium value green: New Gamboge + Winsor Blue + touch of Burnt Umber). When dry, the pupils are Neutral Tint. Now, take a look. Is one eye larger than the other, or are they not completely round? Try outlining them with Neutral Tint on your liner brush.

## CHERRIES

Cherries, yum! I just love them, don't you? You will use some of the same mixes for these cherries that were used for the tin. Mix:

Light Value Red-Orange (Cadmium Red + Cadmium Orange)
Light Value Cadmium Red
Medium Value Red (Alizarin Crimson + Cadmium Red)
Dark Value Alizarin Crimson
Medium Value Navy Blue (Winsor Blue + Brown Madder)

All of the cherries are painted the same way. However, the highlights, and the reflections of the cloth, are different on each cherry. Study your pattern and photo to help you with this. These cherries are in a very strong sunlight. Where the sunlight hits them most strongly, it turns their red color almost orange. With this in mind begin to base them in with the two light value red mixes. Begin at the top with the light value red-orange (don't forget to leave the highlight clean, white paper!) and about a third of the way down switch to light value Cadmium Red to finish basing the cherry. In case your confused, let me clarify: DON'T paint over the white highlight at the top of the cherry, but you DO paint over the light reflections that are lower down on the cherry. Let this dry.

Now, you will begin to form the cherry by leaving the color light at the top, painting it darker in the middle, and even darker along the bottom. Work on dry paper, and this time paint AROUND the reflections. Yes, there will be definite hard edges to define those reflections. Ready? To keep the top edge light use clean water in the tip of the 4 round brush to begin painting there. Then pick up one drop of the medium value Cadmium Red and continue where you left off with the clean water right down to the reflections. When that Cadmium Red hits the clean water it will feather outward making a nice, soft edge of color. Good! Rinse the brush and soften if you wish. Then finish out the darkest areas of the cherry with dark value Alizarin Crimson. The big cherry on the right side of the tin needs an extra dark. That's what the medium value navy blue (Winsor Blue + Brown Madder) is for. Touch a drop of it into the cherry color while it is still wet.

## STEMS

Mix a light value yellow green (New Gamboge + Cobalt Blue). You will also use dark value green (Winsor Blue + Burnt Umber + touch of New Gamboge). Using your liner brush, wet the stems with the light value yellow green. When dry, paint on the dark areas with the dark value green. Finally, the stem on the far left has the woody area showing. That's the part where it was broken off the tree. Simply base that little section with light value Burnt Umber, then dab a spot of Neutral Tint on to darken the lower edge.

## DOILY

This is the doily that is on my daughter Sara's dresser. It has a big heart in the middle of it. Note that the top of the doily remains clean, white paper. Mix a light value Alizarin Crimson. Using the 1 inch brush, take a stroke all along the top of the doily with clean water. Then pick up the light value Alizarin Crimson and take a second stroke just under the first. Continue downward, picking up just a bit more Alizarin Crimson to darken the mix to a medium value, until you've painted all but the white edges all along the bottom edge. Now, look back at the top. If you need to soften the color there, rinse the brush and LIGHTLY stroke over it. Let it dry.

Mix a light value Cobalt Blue and stroke over the doily where it falls over the edge of the table and is in shadow. Once again, let it dry. Then use the same Cobalt Blue mix and your 4 round brush to paint on the tiny lines that show the weave of the doily.

## TABLE

The table is medium value violet brown (Burnt Umber + Winsor Violet). You can see the table through all of the holes in the doily. Just fill in those places, on dry paper, with the brown mix.

## UNDER THE TABLE

Use a dark value navy blue (Winsor Blue + Brown Madder) to fill in those very dark places under the table. If you don't get it dark enough the first time. Let it dry, then apply a second coat. There, finished! I hope that now, these are some of your favorite things, too!

**Matting Suggestions** - Inner Crescent 900, Outer 4405

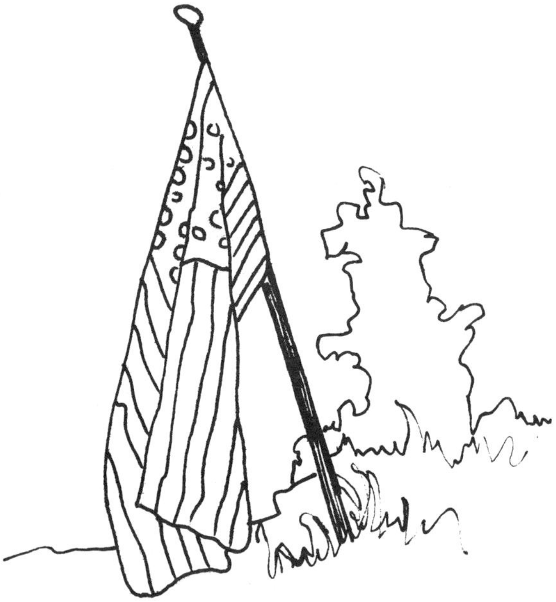

# OLD GLORY

**PAPER SIZE:** 10" x 14"

## PALETTE

Winsor Blue
Cobalt Blue
Payne's Gray
Burnt Umber
Alizarin Crimson
Brown Madder
New Gamboge
Burnt Sienna
Cadmium Red

Transfer this pattern following the instructions at the front of this book.

## PORCH

Let's start right out by defining the porch. It looks like there's a lot to do, but it's really not so bad and a lot of fun! Mix the following:

Medium Value Gray (Winsor Blue + Brown Madder)
Dark Value Black (Winsor Blue + more Brown Madder)
Medium Value Cobalt Blue

Study the porch, and find the section that is in shadow. This part is really the house itself, right? Before beginning to paint, be sure that everything has been transferred to your paper from the pattern. Redefine the lines with a pencil if you have to. Then pick up a bit of medium value gray (Winsor Blue + Brown Madder) in the 8 round brush and begin to fill in the area that is actually the house. Work right on dry paper - and go AROUND THE FERNS, but don't worry about the windows. Go ahead and paint right over them. Paint right on down to the railing. Some of this gray mix is also tucked in between SOME of the posts. Take a look at this for a moment. You cannot see the house behind the posts at the very left, so those are not separated by gray. Also, each post is actually two colors - a strip of clean, white paper and a strip of Cobalt Blue right next to it. So, don't make the posts too skinny. Leave room for both of those things. Let the gray dry, then use dark value black (Winsor Blue + more Brown Madder) to paint in the windows, once again on dry paper. They should only be two or three values darker than the house.

Now, mix up a light value Burnt Umber and fill in the porch floor. Use this mix to also fill in between those posts on the left.

On to the porch itself. Most of the porch remains clean, white paper. Using medium value Cobalt Blue, simply paint on all of the shadows - down the right sides of the columns and underneath the arches, under the roof line, the right sides of all of the posts, and finally, the right sides of the stairway railings and posts. That was easy enough, wasn't it?

**BRICK**

Mix a light value Burnt Sienna and fill in the brick area on the steps. When dry, use a liner to separate them with medium value Cobalt Blue. They also cast a shadow onto the white step underneath them.

**ROOF AND TOP STORY OF THE HOUSE**

Pull a bit of medium value gray (Winsor Blue + Brown Madder). Fill in the entire roof with this mix, and while it is still wet and shiny, dab on a touch of Burnt Umber here and there. Now, mix a dark green of Winsor Blue + Burnt Umber for the shutters. They are done loosely by washing over themlightly with this mix, then going back over the edges with the same mix. Just connect the vertical edges with several horizontal strokes.

The siding is formed only by the shadows that it casts. Mix a bit of the light value gray mix (Winsor Blue + Burnt Umber) in the medium value Cobalt Blue mix. Use that blue-gray color to paint on all of the tiny shadows cast by each piece of siding.

**BACKGROUND TREES**

Mix a light value Burnt Sienna, and dark value green (Winsor Blue + Brown Madder + Cobalt Blue). With clean water, wet from the top of the paper down to the horizon line, being careful to leave the little tree dry. Load the 8 round brush with light value Burnt Sienna. Then lower the handle so that you'll be using the entire side of the brush rather than the tip only. Pull down from the top of the tree line, filling in this entire section. Using an upward stroke here will "push" the trees up into the sky! Quickly, while it's all still wet and SHINY, load dark value green (Winsor Blue + Brown Madder + Cobalt Blue) into the brush and paint only the tree line in the same manner. These trees should soften slightly. If they "explode" up into the sky, quickly squeeze all the water from your brush and use a pressure stroke to wipe back the tops of the trees to where they belong. Never blot when working on wet paper, because this leaves a dry spot that will be evident after the area is dry. (When paint "explodes" like this, it means there's too much water somewhere. First, check the paper - is it evenly shiny, no puddles? If there are puddles, wait for a moment or two before painting. Next, check your mixes. Are they as thick as they're supposed to be? Most likely, here is where the problem lies. Thicken up the mix and try again). There is also a small section of background trees that shows between columns of the porch. Wet the little section with light value Burnt Sienna, then float on the dark green mix as before.

**FERNS AND SMALL TREES**

These three are all painted in the same manner.

Mix: Medium Value Yellow Green (New Gamboge + Payne's Gray)

Dark Value Green (Above mix + more Payne's Gray)

In each case, wet the entire area...that is, the entire fern or tree. Use the 4 round brush and pick up medium value yellow green (New Gamboge + Payne's Gray). Dab it pretty much over the entire area. The dark value green (New Gamboge + more Payne's Gray) must be place more carefully, however. Once again, use a small brush and pick up only a drop or two of color in the tip. Think of where the highlights are. For example, the tree is highlighted on the top left side. So, the dark will go elsewhere. Same way with the ferns. Leave lots of light. You can always go back and add more dark if you need it.

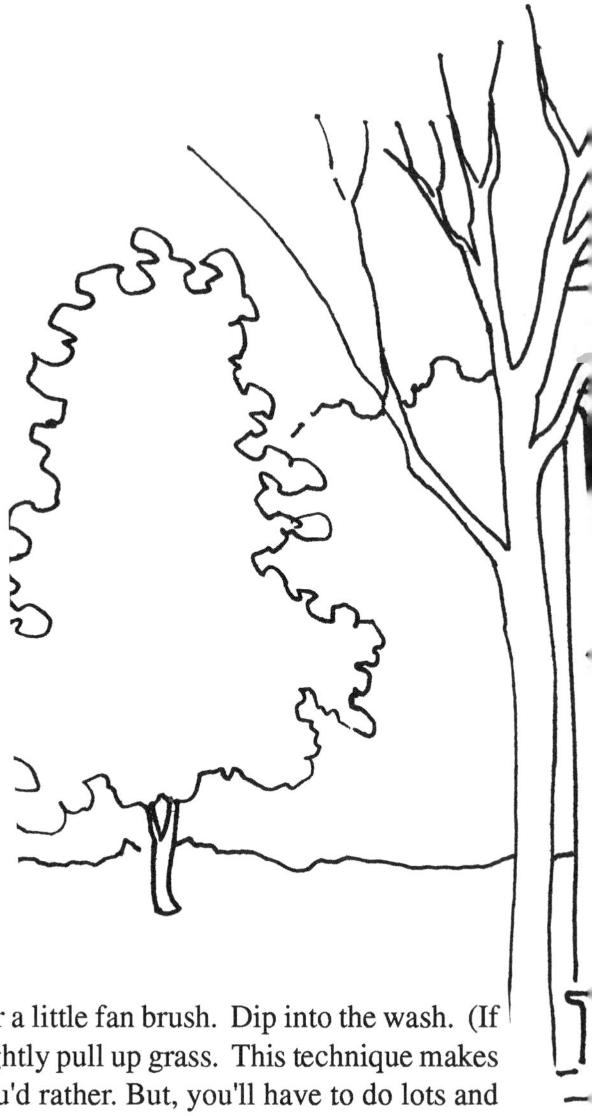

Using a light value Burnt Umber, wash in the Walk Way. When dry, wet the entire lower section of the paper. While still wet, float light value yellow green (New Gamboge + Payne's Gray) onto the ground area around the small tree. Then bring it on down across the front of the house. Pick up dark value green (New Gamboge + more Payne's Gray) and stroke here and there HORIZONTALLY. This color will soften out. Let it dry.

Now, let's make it look like grass. Use a rake brush if you have one. If not, dampen your 8 round brush and squeeze all of the water out in a kleenex. Pinch the bristles at the ferrule to spread them out until your brush looks like a rake, or a little fan brush. Dip into the wash. (If it closes up, you have too much wash in it, try again). Now, lightly pull up grass. This technique makes the grass look "thicker". You can just use a liner brush, if you'd rather. But, you'll have to do lots and lots of liner grass to make it look the same.

**LARGE DEAD TREE**

Do a small section of the tree at a time - only as much as you feel comfortable with. Wet the section with light value Burnt Sienna. While it is still wet, stroke medium value gray (Winsor Blue + Brown Madder) onto the right side., Allow it to blend out as it wishes. Quickly, get a stylus (or sharp pencil) and draw short vertical lines right onto the tree trunk. What happens here is the stylus scores the paper, and the color runs into the line. It makes nice looking bark. Continue working your way up the tree, drying before going on to the next section. Finally, at the top use a liner and a light value gray (Winsor Blue + Brown Madder) to simply draw on branches.

**OLD GLORY**

Mix these colors:

Light Value Cadmium Red
Medium Value Cadmium Red + Alizarin Crimson
Dark Value Navy Blue (Winsor Blue + Brown Madder)

The flag is draped so that parts of it are folded over. Remember that a section that is in the back

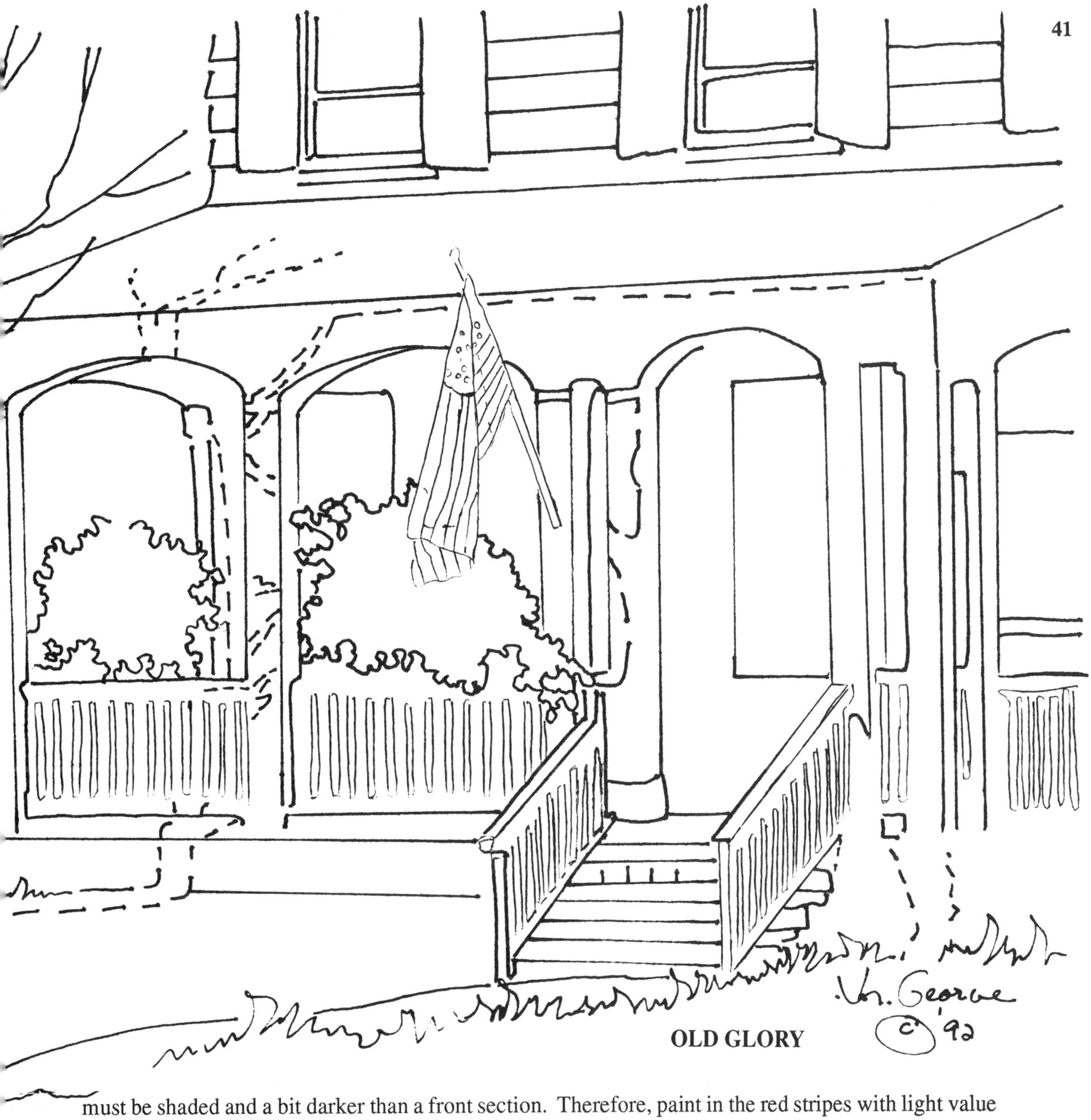


**OLD GLORY**

must be shaded and a bit darker than a front section. Therefore, paint in the red stripes with light value Cadmium Red. Even the red stripes on the back sections are based in with light value Cadmium Red, but then medium value Cadmium Red it touched to it, just where the stripe goes behind a front section. The blue section is dark value navy blue (Winsor Blue + Brown Madder). Don't forget to paint around all of those fifty stars! -- Ha! Just Kidding!! Instead, leave a few white spots and it will give the appearance of the stars on the flag. OR - fill the area in completely with dark value navy blue, then pick them out later with a scratch knife blade or X-acto. Paint the pole with light value Burnt Sienna and line the left side with a gray mix. Finally, place the cast shadows onto the flag. They are marked on your pattern with a dotted line. Do them with the tip of the 4 round brush and medium value Cobalt Blue. All done!

**Matting Suggestions:** Outer - Crescent 3297, Inner - Crescent 1046

# TWO POTS IN THE WINDOW

**PAPER SIZE:** 15" x 22"

**PALETTE**
Cobalt Blue
Brown Madder
Winsor Blue
Alizarin Crimson
Payne's Gray
Burnt Umber
Burnt Sienna
Raw Sienna
New Gamboge
Prussian Blue

Transfer the pattern following directions at the front of this book.

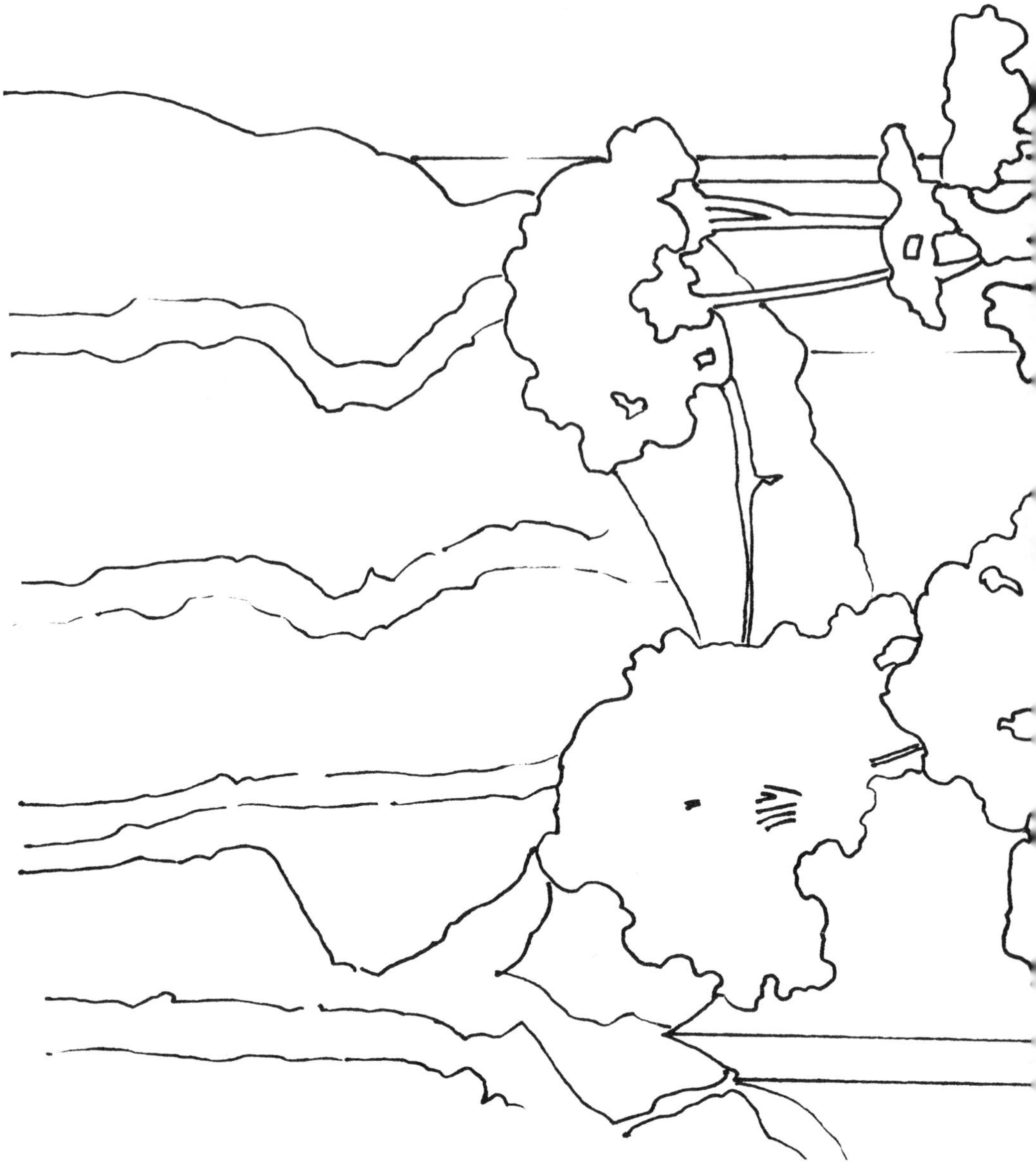

**CURTAIN**

Begin by mixing a large puddle of medium value blue (Cobalt Blue + a touch of Burnt Umber). Fully load the 1 inch brush with this mix and paint one section of the curtain at a time, using less color on the light areas and dabbing extra color on the darker places. Let it dry, then rewet and float on even more color if you need it. While this is drying, mix a bit of medium value navy blue (Winsor Blue + Brown Madder). See in between the sections where the folds are very dark? Use the navy mix there. It's put right onto dry paper, and look, it isn't even smooth looking. Make the outside edges crisp and neat, then just wiggle the brush around to fill in the inside. Then, pick up a bit of the medium value blue (Cobalt Blue + touch of Burnt Umber) in the tip of the 8 round brush and, on dry paper, paint on all of the markings you see on the curtain. Only the vertical ones are given for you on the pattern. Study the photo to help you with this. Don't worry, it's really easy! It doesn't have to be exactly like mine.

**WINDOW FRAME**

First mix these gray mixes:
Light Value Blue Gray (Cobalt + Burnt Umber)
Light Value Violet Gray (Above mix + touch Alizarin Crimson)

**Pattern continues on pages 46-47**

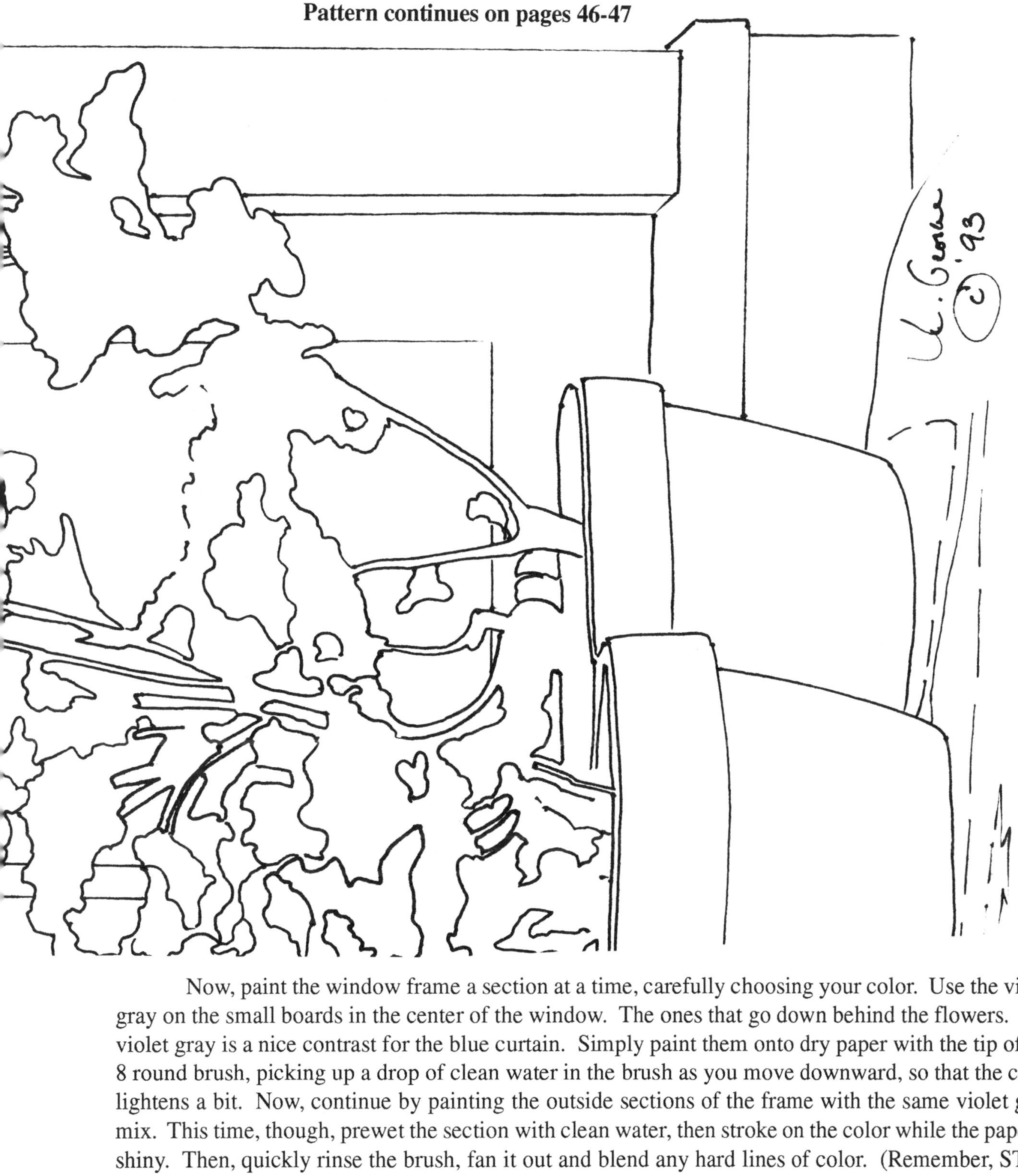

Now, paint the window frame a section at a time, carefully choosing your color. Use the violet gray on the small boards in the center of the window. The ones that go down behind the flowers. The violet gray is a nice contrast for the blue curtain. Simply paint them onto dry paper with the tip of the 8 round brush, picking up a drop of clean water in the brush as you move downward, so that the color lightens a bit. Now, continue by painting the outside sections of the frame with the same violet gray mix. This time, though, prewet the section with clean water, then stroke on the color while the paper is shiny. Then, quickly rinse the brush, fan it out and blend any hard lines of color. (Remember, STOP BLENDING WHILE THE PAPER STILL HAS A SHINE or you will simply make things worse. Once the paper has lost the shine, each time you touch the brush to the paper it picks up paint and makes a streak)!

When all of that has dried, move on to the inner sections of the window frame. For these, switch to the light value blue gray (Cobalt Blue + Burnt Umber) to help separate them from the other sections. Once again, prewet the section first to make the blending easier. Take a quick look at the photo and find the section just above the right pot. If you study it, you'll see that you prewet that particular area with light value Raw Sienna and then floated on the blue gray shading color. Let it all dry.

## WALL AND TABLE

The areas to the right and left of the window are wall. The wall also extends just slightly below the window, and very subtly becomes a table. There are really no sharp lines there. The wall color simply, slowly becomes table color. So, here's how to do it. Mix a light value Brown Madder + Burnt Umber. You will also use the light value Raw Sienna mix. Using the 1 inch brush, begin on one side of the window and stroke downward with the Brown Madder + Burnt Umber mix. Keep moving, and when you begin to go under the window, rinse the brush and pick up light value Raw Sienna. Use the Raw Sienna all the way across underneath the window, then switch back to the Brown Madder + Burnt Umber mix and finish up on the other side of the window. Now, take a look at the wall color. Is it O.K., or is it too bright? Soften it down by letting it dry, re-wetting, then floating on one of the light value gray mixes used in the window frame. Let it dry.

## POTS

The pots will be painted one at a time, allowing each one to dry before starting on the other. Note that the pot to the right is much darker, and so has a lot more shadow color. Mix:

Medium Value Rust (Brown Madder + Burnt Sienna)
Dark Value Rust (Brown Madder + Burnt Sienna + Winsor Blue)
Dark Value Navy Blue (Winsor Blue + Brown Madder)

Each pot has two sections, the lip and the main section underneath. Working on the front pot first, wet the lip with clean water, then stroke on the medium value rust (Brown Madder + Burnt Sienna). Let this color be a bit darker on the right side because the light is blocked there by the other pot. When it has dried, wet the other section of the pot with the medium value rust mix. While it's still wet and SHINY stroke on the dark value rust just under the lip, along the entire bottom and up the right side, leaving a light highlighted spot on the left. When totally dry, place a cast shadow into the lip with the medium value rust (Brown Madder + Burnt Sienna). Now for the other pot.

Once again, do the lip and the main section separately. Fill in the lip of this pot with the dark value rust (Brown Madder + Burnt Sienna + Winsor Blue). Let it dry, then prewet the bottom section with the medium value rust mix. While wet, stroke dark value rust under the lip and onto the left side. Allow it to dry, then rewet that bottom section and apply a bit of dark value navy blue (Winsor Blue + Brown Madder) under the lip and along the left edge to further separate the two pots. Then thin a bit of the dark value navy blue to a medium value and paint the insides of the pots. Just use the tip of the 4 round brush and paint around the stems that will later be sticking up out of the pot. Also notice that the edges of the pots remain clean, white paper!

With a light value Alizarin Crimson also a medium value red (Alizarin Crimson + Cadmium Red). How you paint the flowers will have a great effect on the amount of light that appears to be coming into the window. Try standing in front of really bright light. You'll see that sometimes the light is so bright that objects in front of it almost seem to disappear! Therefore, those flowers that are directly in front of the window will be much light than those that are behind the curtain a bit. Paint them on dry paper, filling in with the lightest value of Alizarin Crimson, and while still wet dab on bits of extra color towards the center.

## PEACH

Base in the peach with a medium value of Raw Sienna, and while it's still wet dab medium value rust (Brown Madder + Burnt Sienna) along the bottom. Rinse the brush, then soften any hard edges.

## LEAVES

Mix the following greens:

Light Value Yellow Green (New Gamboge + touch Payne's Gray)

Medium Value Green (above mix + more Payne's Gray)

Dark Value Blue Green (Winsor Blue + Burnt Umber + Prussian Blue)

Don't let all of these leaves worry you! They're not as hard as they look. Let's simplify - break them up into two different types - light leaves and dark leaves. Start by using the lightest value, light value yellow green (New Gamboge + touch of Payne's Gray) to lightly wash over the entire main body of the leaves. Let this dry thoroughly. Continue by painting in the leaves all around the outside of the group. These are separate, individual leaves that should be easy for you to pick out, and they're all painted in the same manner. Prewet with the lightest value green, then dab on one of the darker value greens to shade. As with the geraniums, those leaves that are directly in front of the window stay very light and are not shaded with a darker green. Now, study the pattern and photo to aid you in painting the next step. You will be using "negative painting". That simply means that instead of painting the leaves themselves, you'll be painting the spaces around them. Either of the two darker mixes of green may be used. The best way to do this is to start in one spot and work your way across. Don't skip around, that's too confusing. Work on dry paper using whichever brush you feel comfortable with, and take your time. Just fill in each little area with paint. If this is your first time doing this, try penciling X's in the leaves to help you know which places don't get painted dark. In any case, always paint what makes sense to you. Don't be afraid to change any part of the pattern!

## SHADOWS

The shadows of the pots are based in with the medium value rust (Brown Madder + Burnt Sienna), and while still wet and shiny dab dark value navy blue (Winsor Blue + Brown Madder) right up next to the pots. So, the shadows should be darker right up under the pots and get lighter as they move outward.

There are light little shadows suggested for some of the leaves and the peach. Using the light value blue gray (Cobalt Blue + touch Burnt Umber), scribble a few light, washy shadows that connect to the leaves along the table top. There, you're done!

**Matting Suggestions:**

Outside, Crescent 1615 Inside, Crescent 973

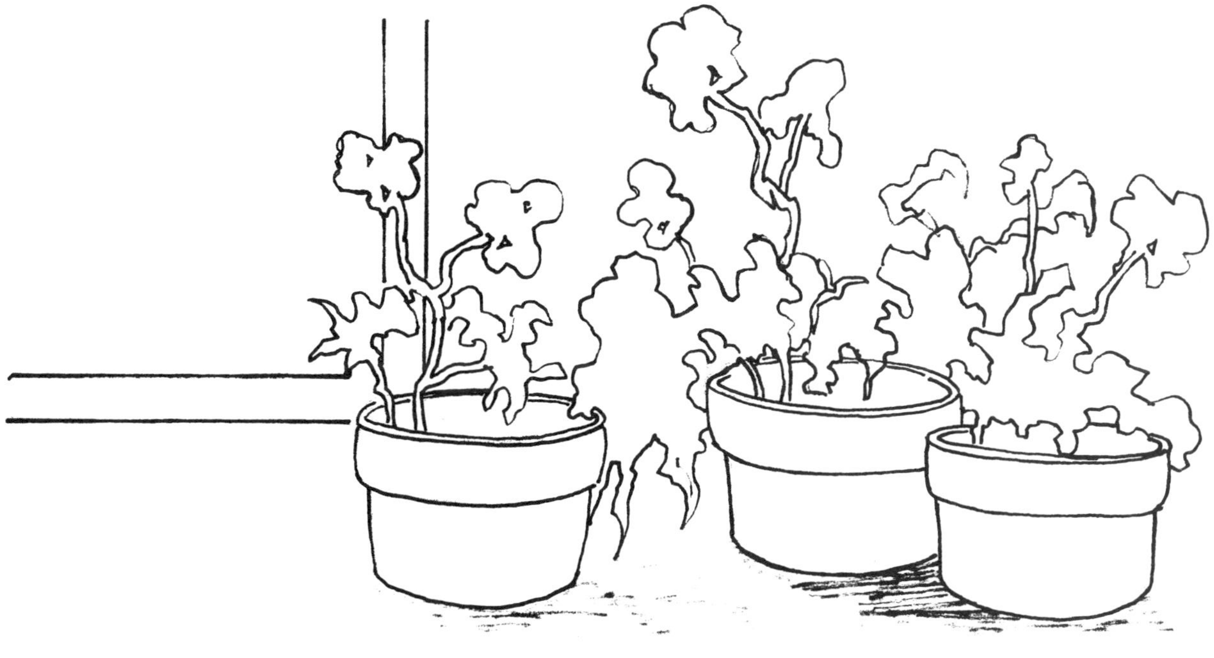

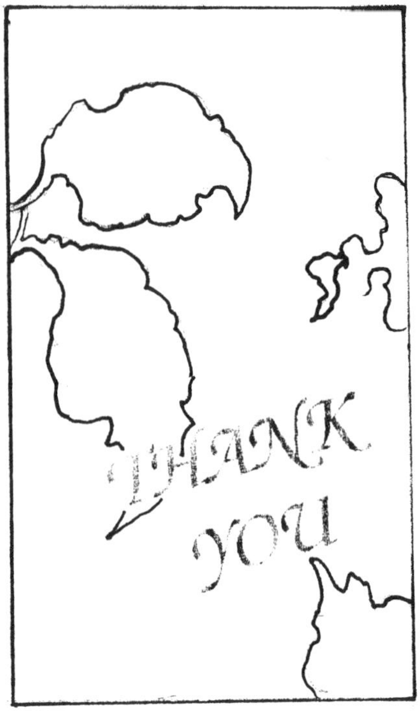


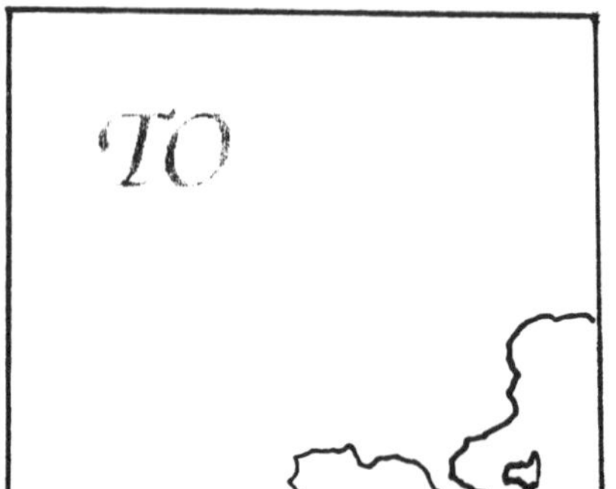


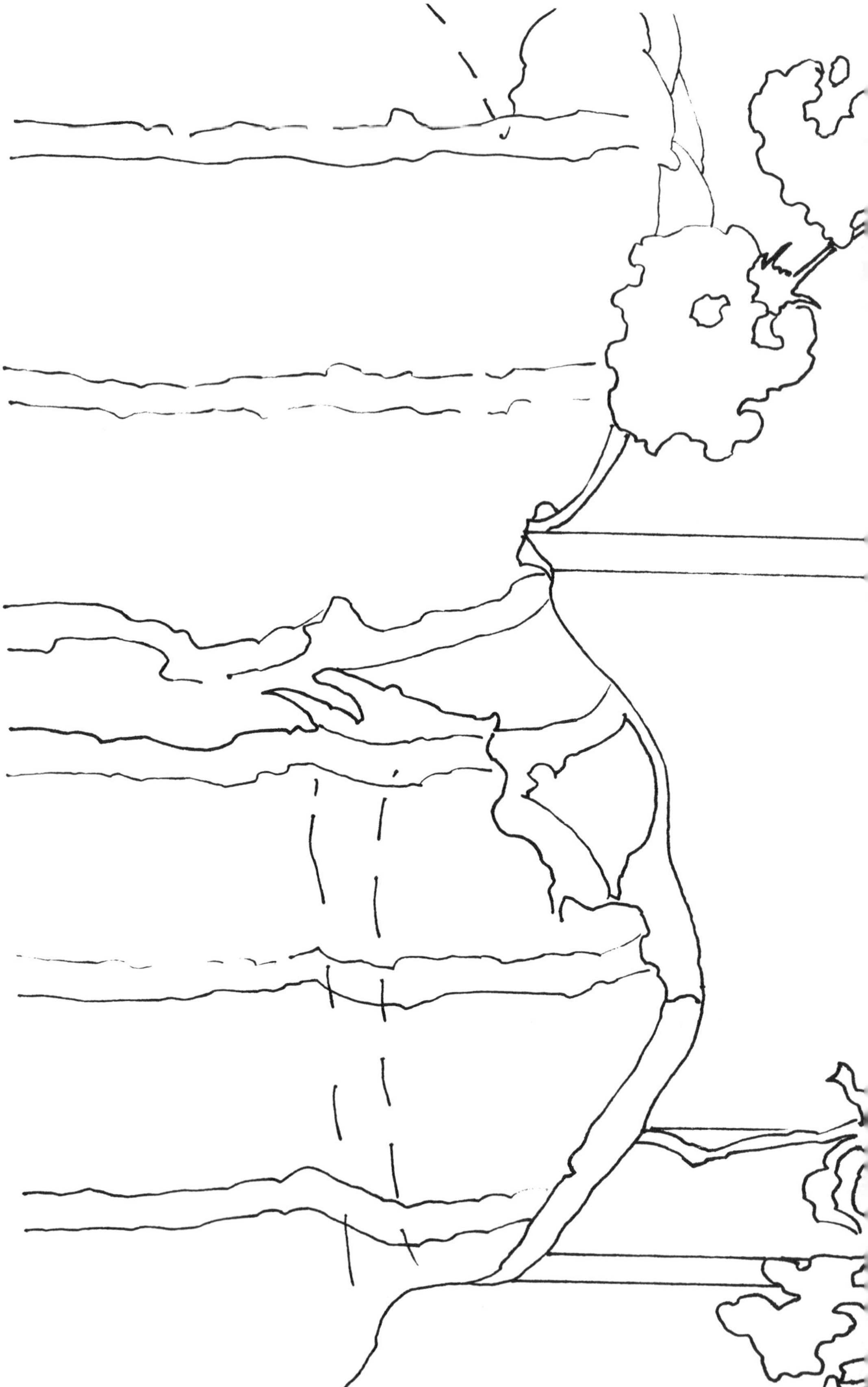

TWO POTS IN THE WINDOW

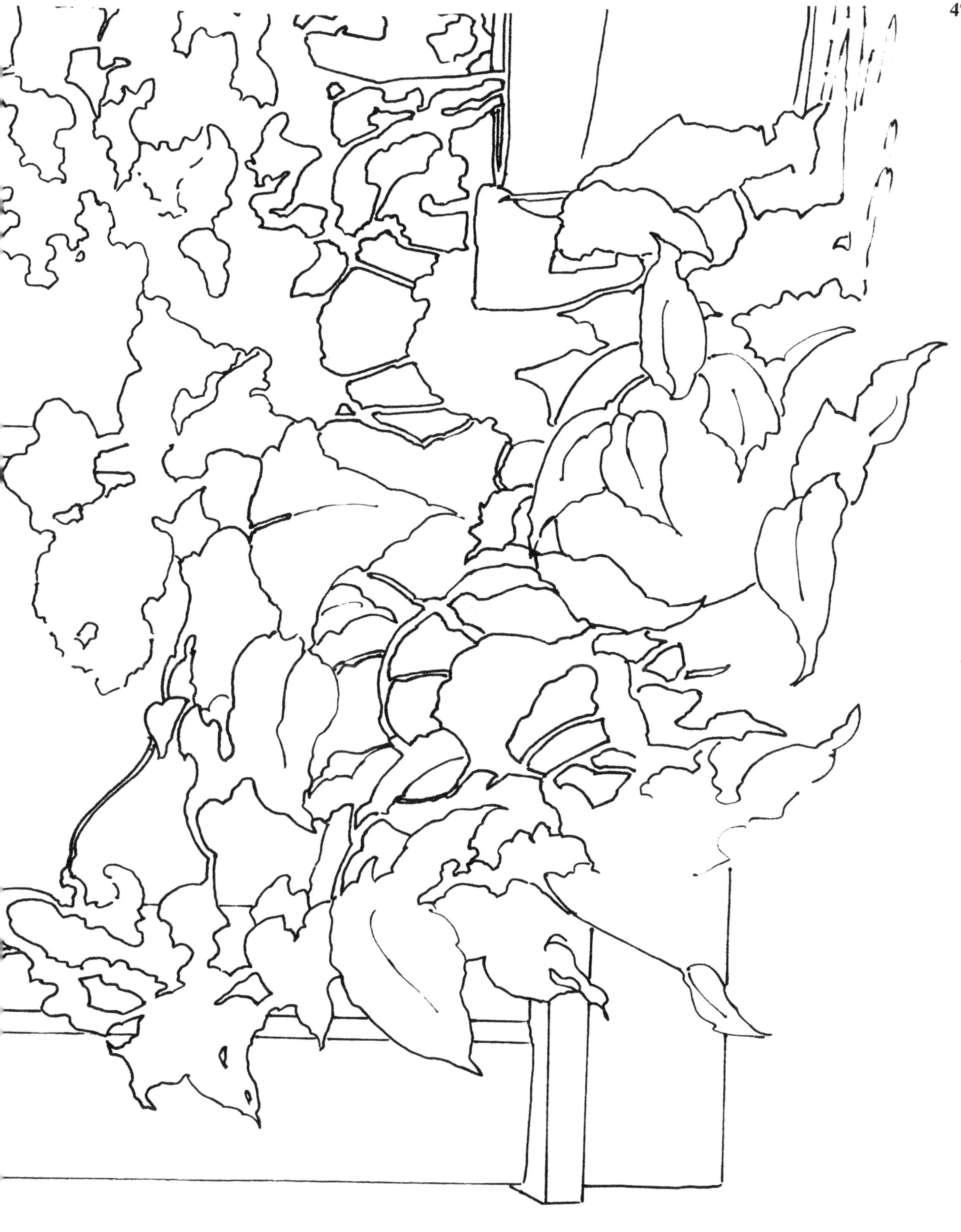

## SUMMER MEMORY

**PAPER SIZE:** 8-1/2" x 14"

**PALETTE**

Ultramarine Blue
Winsor Blue
Prussian Blue
Burnt Sienna
Burnt Umber
Raw Sienna
Winsor Violet

Transfer the pattern following the instructions at the front of this book.

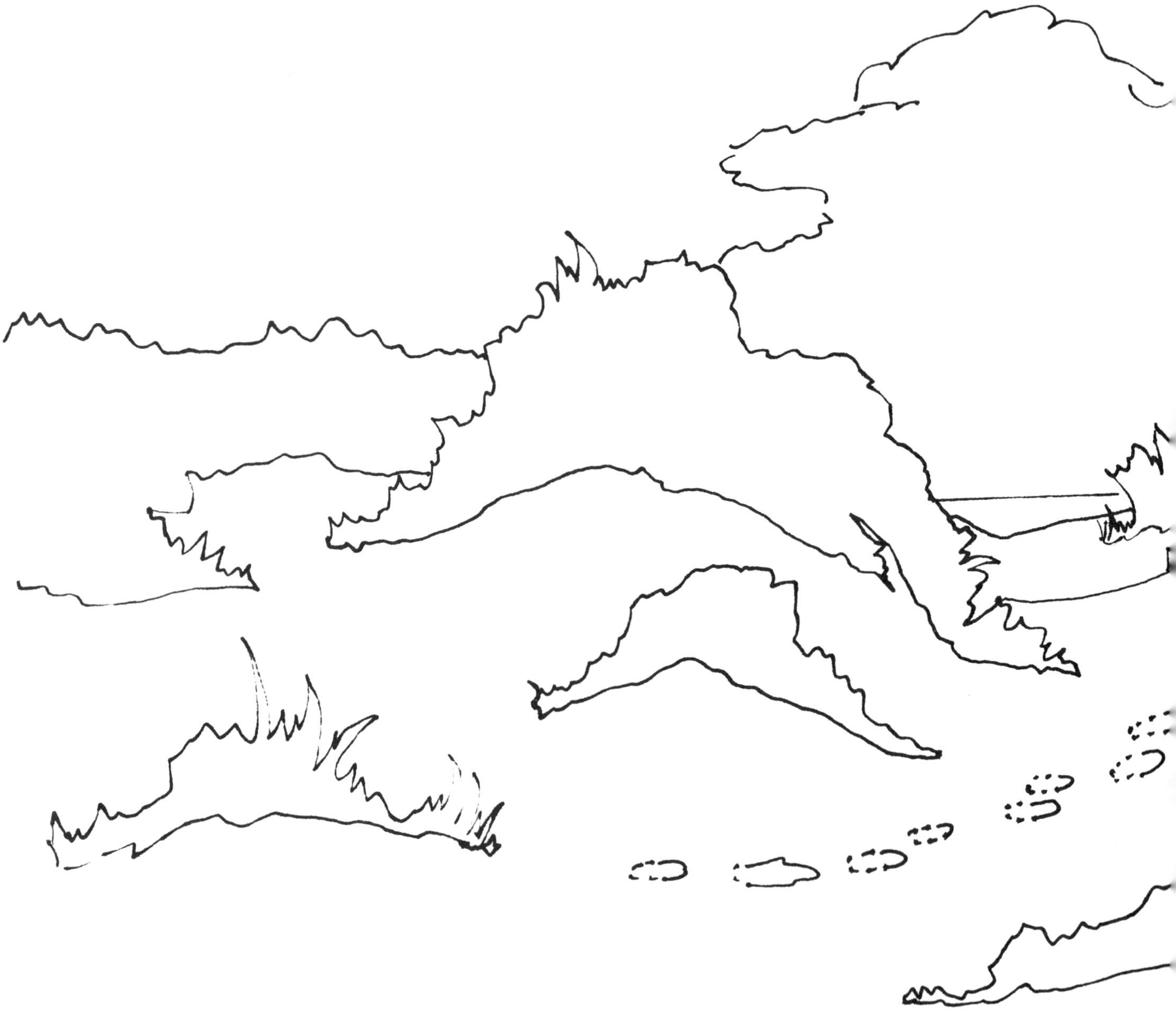

**SKY**

Mix these color mixes for the sky:

Medium Value Blue )Ultramarine Blue + touch Burnt Umber)
Dark Value Blue Green (Prussian Blue + Burnt Umber)
Dark Value Navy Blue (Winsor Blue + Brown Madder)

You're probably asking yourself, is there a "Trick" to this sky? Yes, there is! That "trick" is to lay the color on and not play with it. I know that sounds too simple, but it really is. Just put the color on and allow the water to do wonderful things with it. Ready to try? Good!

**SUMMER MEMORY**

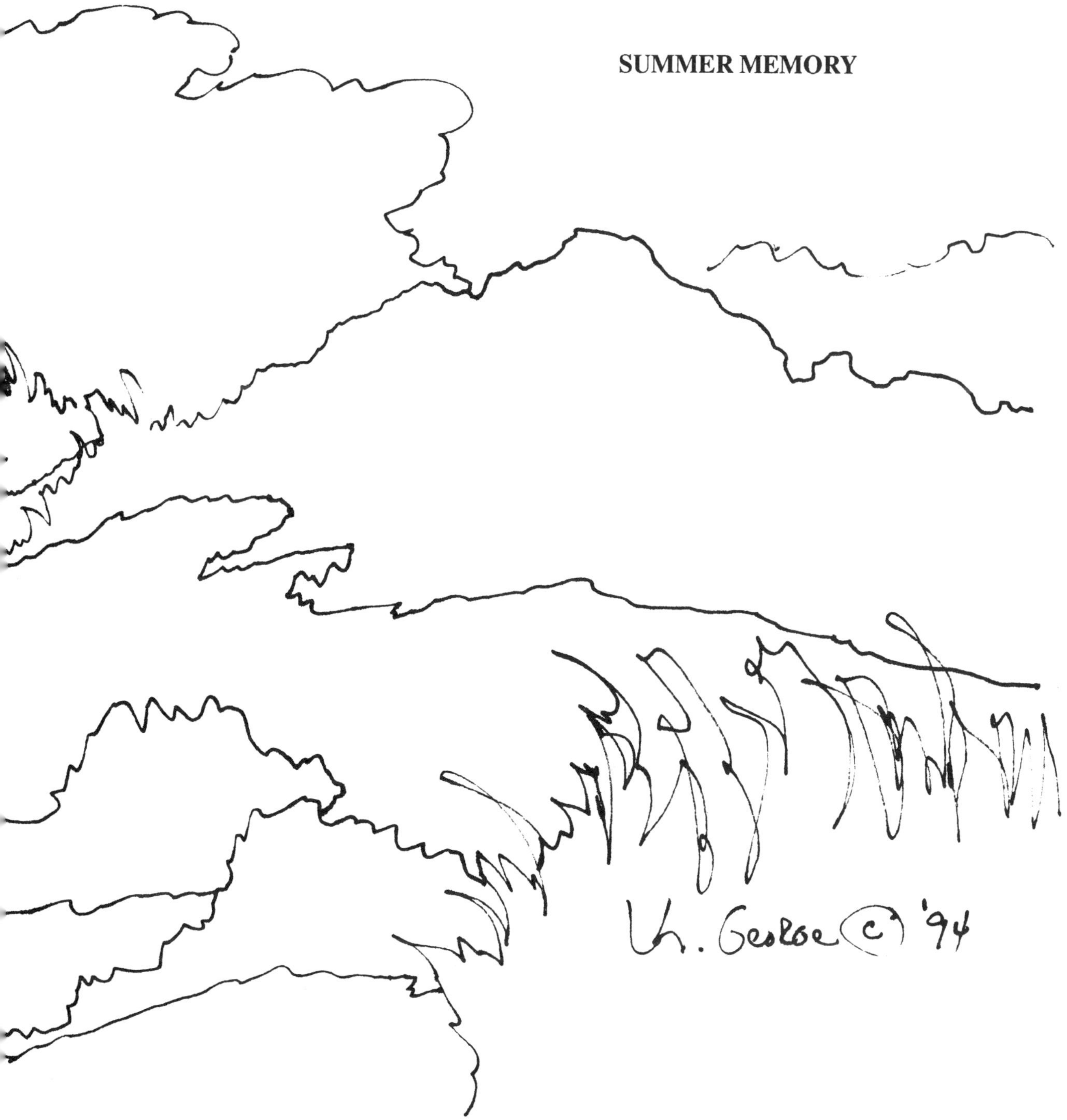

Wet the entire sky area, from the horizon line to the top of the paper. Look for a nice, even shine - no puddles and no dry spots. The basic color of this sky is medium value blue (Ultramarine Blue + Burnt Umber). The other two colors are used just to darken the sky. So, pick up the medium value blue with the 1" brush. Use a short, choppy stroke to lay the color onto the sky. Set the brush down first where the color is the darkest, then continue to set the brush down in short, choppy strokes all across the sky. Be sure and leave that nice, clean white area in the center. (Remember now, as long as the paper is wet the color will continue to spread out, so leave the white spot larger than you actually want it to be)! Next, check the paper...is it still wet? If not, please stop, let it dry completely, then rewet before doing the next step! If you paper IS still evenly shiny, go ahead and darken the corners with one, or both, of the other two mixes.

**DUNES**

There are only two color mixes used to paint the dunes. They are:

Medium Value Burnt Sienna
Dark Value Violet Brown (Burnt Umber + Winsor Violet)

Begin by painting the tiny little section of dune just below the water. Wet that little section and touch just a drop of the dark value violet brown (Burnt Umber + Winsor Violet) all along the bottom edge. Then, quickly rinse the brush, fan it a bit and soften the top edge of color away to nothing. When that has dried, go ahead and wet the entire bottom of the paper, from the horizon line down. Work with either the 8 round or the 1" brush, whichever feels most comfortable to you today, and pick up medium value Burnt Sienna. Take a look at the photo to see how the dunes are formed. They are shaded on both sides with a lighter area through the middle. Therefore, set the brush down to one side of that light center area and push the paint outward. This will help keep that center area light. If you stroke inward, you will also "push" the paint inward and it will be more likely to float over your light section. Lightly cover the dunes with the medium value Burnt Sienna, then darken the areas at the base of the grasses with dark value violet brown (Burnt Umber + Winsor Violet). Allow the color to float out and soften as it wishes. If you think that too much color has floated into the light area, just rinse the brush, blot it and use a pressure stroke to wipe back unwanted paint. Don't blot! Blotting leaves a dry spot, but because a damp brush still contains moisture, wiping back paint will look much softer. You can even blend a bit if you see any hard lines of color forming. Be sure that your brush has all of the water squeezed out of it, though. Then fan it, and place it half on the color and half off of it and lightly blend. Let this dry thoroughly.

**FOOTPRINTS**

If you look carefully at that light center section of the dunes, you'll notice some tiny footprints in the sand. These are very easy to paint. Do one at a time, though. Wet it carefully with clean water, then touch the right side of each with one tiny drop of medium value violet brown (Burnt Umber + Winsor Violet) in the tip of the 4 round brush. This color will immediately start to spread outward. So, rinse the brush, blot it and fan it a bit, and lightly soften the left edge of the color to nothing.

**GRASSES**

Mix the following greens for the grasses:

Medium Value Green (Winsor Blue + Burnt Umber + Raw Sienna)
Dark Value Blue Green (Winsor Blue + Burnt Umber)
Dark Value Blue Green (Prussian Blue + Burnt Umber + Winsor Blue)

Before you start anything, check to be sure that everything you have painted up until now is thoroughly dry. Why? Well, you are about to rewet part of the paper and if anything is damp it will float all around, and you will be SO unhappy! Once the paper has dried, the pigment is usually "set" into the paper. Even so, certain ones will still float free once in a while, so use a very light stroke when you rewet. Sometimes, I'll even use a spray bottle to do the job.

All of the grasses (except for the clump on the bottom right corner) are painted the same way, but make it easy on yourself and do only one section at a time. Prewet the paper around the section with clean water. Wet AT LEAST an extra two inches around the clump. This not only gives you more time to work, but plenty of room for the grass to grow upward. Once the paper is wet, check to see if there is a slight shine. If so, you're ready to put on the paint. Start with medium value green (Winsor Blue + Burnt Umber + Raw Sienna) in the 8 round brush. At this point, you're not sure exactly what that paint is going to do when you touch the brush to the paper, so pick up just a drop in the tip of the brush. (the more paint in the brush, the less control you will have). Touch the brush at the base of the grass and stroke upward. Tilt the handle of the brush down slightly so that you'll be using more the side of the brush rather than the tip. The color should hold its shape, but soften slightly. If it is doing that, keep on going and fill in the entire area. Then go back in here and there with the darker green mixes. But what if you touched the brush to the paper and color "exploded" outward? That just means that there is too much water somewhere. First, check the paper - is it evenly shiny? If so, then the paper is fine. Try blotting extra water from the brush by touching a kleenex to the ferrule. Then, try again. It should be much better this time. Chances are, if the paint explodes you either picked up too much paint with your brush, or your paint mix is too thin.

These first washes are just a background for the grass. Now you can add details, and even more color, if you wish. A rake brush works great for this. If you don't have one, use your 8 round brush. (For extra help, see "Drybrushing" at the front of this book). Using the two darker green mixes only, pull up lots of grass. Then switch to a liner brush, and pull up lots (and lots) of liner grasses. They're being blown by the wind and sway ever so softly to the left. TIP: Your grass will be much more natural looking if you end it gradually rather than stop it suddenly. See how each "finger" of grass gets smaller and smaller on the end, until there's nothing there but a few liner grasses. Try to end with those small grasses rather than tall ones.

As a final step, glaze some of the grass with a medium value Winsor Violet. Just brush it right over the grass. This adds a spark to it. If you don't like it, just blot it off with a paper towel while it's still wet.

**GRASS AT BOTTOM RIGHT CORNER**

This kind of grass is really fun to do! Use the same grass mixes you have already mixed:

Dark Value Green (Winsor Blue + Burnt Umber)

Dark Value Blue Green (Prussian Blue + Burnt Umber + Winsor Blue)

Prewet the entire bottom corner, upward enough to give the grass room to grow. While still shiny, stroke on the grass washes using the 1" brush. This should be quite dark at this point. You're going to scrape out the grasses with the handle of your 1" inch brush. But you have to be patient and wait for just the right time to do it - when the paper is just about to lose the shine. Don't worry, you'll be able to tell! Tilt the handle of the 1 inch brush slightly so that you're using a bit of the side, not the very tip. Then use a slow, steady movement to scrape out some of the paint. That, in fact, is what you are doing. You are scraping out the grasses. Be sure that they curve gracefully to the left, as the other grasses do. Wait until this is dry, then add liner grass of the same colors to really make this spot look nice. Finally, glaze over it if you wish with the medium value Winsor Violet.

**WATER**

You may want to double check that the top of the water line is absolutely straight. Use a ruler to be sure. Wet the tiny section of water with medium value Ultramarine Blue. While it is still wet, pick up a drop of dark value blue green (Prussian Blue + Burnt Umber + Winsor Blue) in the liner brush and touch it to the left side. Let it float out a bit and soften.

**Matting Suggestions:** Crescent 908, Inner, Bainbridge 46B

**COMPLIMENTARY PAIR**

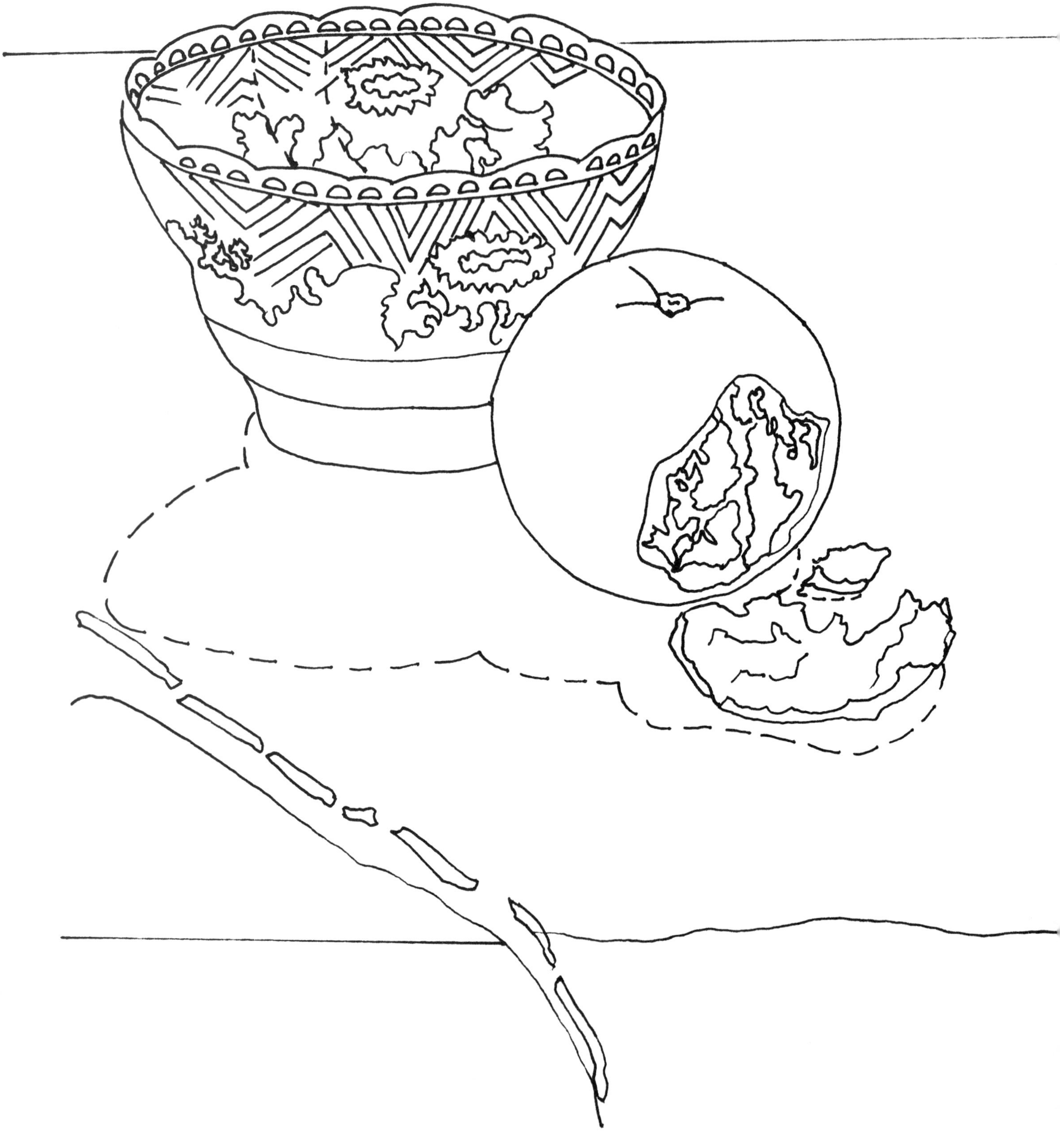

## COMPLIMENTARY PAIR

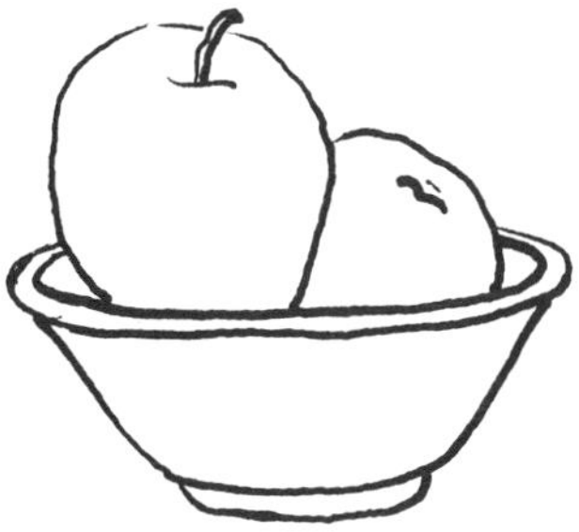

**PAPER SIZE:** 10" x 11"

**PALETTE**

| | |
|---|---|
| Cadmium Orange | Alizarin Crimson |
| Brown Madder | Cobalt Blue |
| Cobalt Violet | Ultramarine Blue |
| Burnt Sienna | Winsor Violet |
| New Gamboge | Raw Sienna |

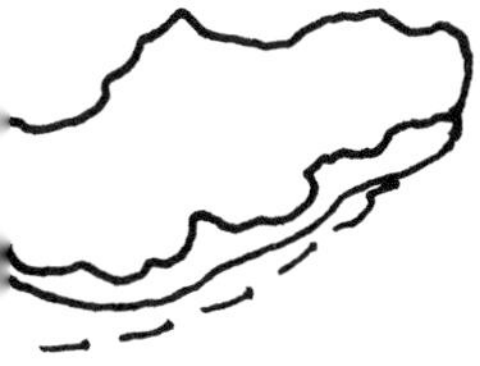

Transfer the pattern following the instructions at the front of this book.

**ORANGE**

Mix Light Value Cadmium Orange
Medium Value Cadmium Orange
Medium Value Red (Alizarin Crimson + Brown Madder)

Begin by wetting the outside of the orange (do not paint the sections that show the inside of the orange) with light value Cadmium Orange. Be sure that it is evenly wet and SHINY. Pink up a small amount of medium value Cadmium Orange in the tip of the 8 round brush and stroke it onto the main section of the orange. Do not place it directly on the left edge - move in just a bit. There is reflected light on that left edge that causes it to be lighter. Rinse the brush and soften any hard edges of color. You may have to do this two or three times to reach the color that you want. That's perfectly all right! Just be sure to let each coat dry thoroughly, and to rewet with very clean water. After you have the color how you want it, rewet on final time and dab on a touch of the medium value red (Alizarin Crimson + Brown Madder) right where you want the orange to be the darkest. Let all of this dry thoroughly. Paint in the "thingy" at the top of the orange. (What is that thing called anyway)? Using a light value yellow green (New Gamboge + Cobalt Blue), fill it in on dry paper. When dry, darken the left and bottom edges with dark value Burnt Umber + Ultramarine Blue. Also, put a spot of this dark color in the center. Then let it dry thoroughly.

That "thingy" causes an indentation in the orange, and some shading can be done to form those indentations. They are shown by lines on your pattern. Do each one separately. Wet above the line, and use the liner brush to place a tiny bit of medium value Cadmium Orange just above that line. Then use the damp 4 round brush to soften the top edge of color, if needed. The bottom edge of the color should remain a sharp line.

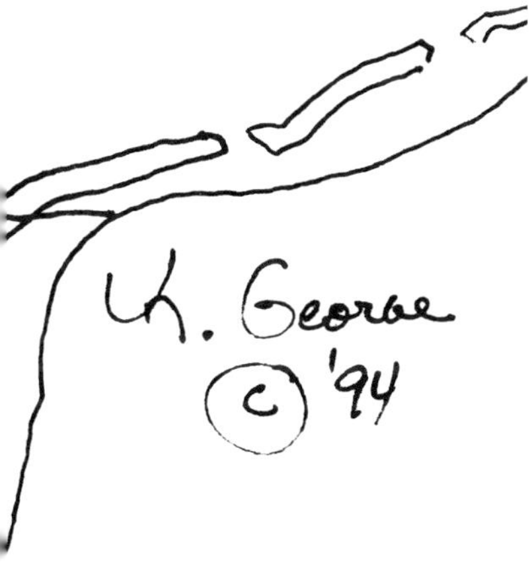


**INSIDE**

Base in the inside section, as well as the pieces of peeling lying on the table, with light value Raw Sienna. Use the 4 round brush and light value Cadmium Orange to fill in the darker areas of the inside, even dab a bit extra on one or two. When dry, rewet the inside, just along the left and bottom and touch it with one drop of medium value red (Alizarin Crimson + Brown Madder) to shade.

Paint the outside of the pieces of peeling with medium Cadmium Orange. When dry, wet the inside of the peelings, and apply medium value Raw Sienna on here and there to add texture.

**BOWL**

Here are the mixtures used on the bowl:

Light Value Cobalt Blue
Medium Value Cobalt Blue
Medium Value Violet (Winsor Violet + Ultramarine Blue + Burnt Sienna)

Beginning with the inside of the bowl, fill in the blue area with light value Cobalt Blue. Let it dry, then apply one more coat over all but the light reflection area that is indicated with a dotted line on the pattern. While this is drying, base in the blue section on the outside of the bowl with medium value Cobalt Blue.

When it has all dried thoroughly, shade the inside. On the inside of the bowl, fill in the entire area to the left of that reflection with light value violet (Winsor Violet + Ultramarine Blue + Burnt Sienna). Then, carefully wet the rest of the inside of the bowl (to the right of the reflection) with clean water. Dab just a touch of the violet right up next to that reflection and let it soften out to the right. The right portion of the inside of the bowl should remain clean and without shading color!

Now, to shade the outside. Carefully wet the outside with clean water and float medium value violet (Winsor Violet + Ultramarine Blue + Burnt Sienna) just behind the orange. This is where the shading should be the darkest. Soften it out toward the left, so that the left portion of the outside of the bowl remains clean and free of shading color. When dry, shade the bottom of the bowl. There are two funny little dips in the bowl. Wet each, one at a time, and float shading color just along the top edge of the wet area. Rinse the brush, and soften the bottom edge of the color to nothing.

Now you may begin to paint on all of the little markings on the bowl. I know, it looks difficult, but it's not. Use your liner brush and medium value Cobalt Blue and simply paint them onto dry paper. If you wish make your own design. Anything will do. Fill in those half circles around the top of the bowl also with medium value Cobalt Blue.

Wash over the rim, here and there, with a light value Burnt Sienna to give it that worn look.

**SHADOW**

Medium Value Blue Gray (Ultramarine Blue + Burnt Sienna)
Medium Value Gray Violet (Winsor Violet + touch medium value Blue gray from above)

Before painting, wet the shadow area with clean water. Look for a slight shine. Then pick up a medium value blue gray (Ultramarine Blue + Burnt Sienna) and begin painting right up next to the bowl and the orange. Gradually fill in the shadow area, switching to the medium value gray violet (Winsor Violet + touch medium value blue gray) as you work outward.

**BACKGROUND**

On dry paper, use the 1 inch brush and fill in the background with light value yellow green (New Gamboge + Cobalt Blue).

**TABLE**

The table can be divided into three sections: the top, and the two lower sections. Wet the top section with clean water, then touch medium value yellow green (New Gamboge + Cobalt Blue) next to the tablecloth. Let it float outward slightly, then soften any hard edges of color.

Both bottom sections are painted the same way. Wet the section with medium value yellow green (New Gamboge + Cobalt Blue). While it is still wet and shiny, stroke on medium value blue gray

(Ultramarine Blue + Burnt Sienna). Once you float on the color, leave it alone and let it blend itself. Ultramarine Blue is a "sedimentary" color. That means it will have this great granulated look - if youdon't mess too much after you apply it.

**TABLECLOTH**

Be sure the table is dry. You will use the bowl mixes to paint the shadow on the tablecloth. They are:

Medium Value Cobalt Blue
Medium Value Violet (Winsor Violet + Ultramarine Blue + Burnt Sienna)

Wet the tablecloth where it hangs over the edge of the table. Then float on the shading colors, first one, then a bit of the other. Let the colors mingle as they wish for a clean, fresh look. When it's dry, paint the stripe onto the cloth with a light value Alizarin Crimson.

**Matting Suggestions:** Outside - Bainbridge 3315, Inside - Bainbridge 3324

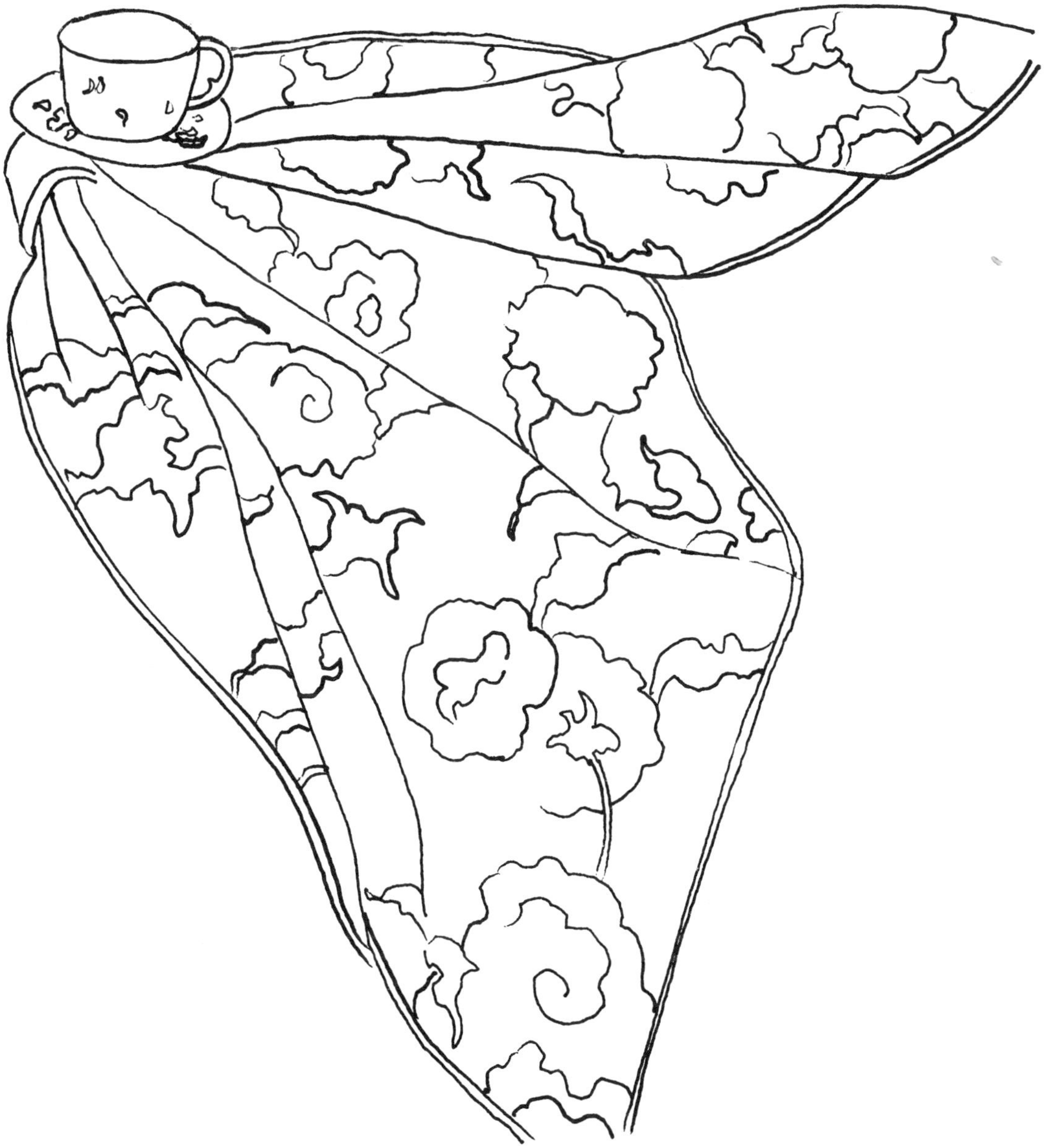

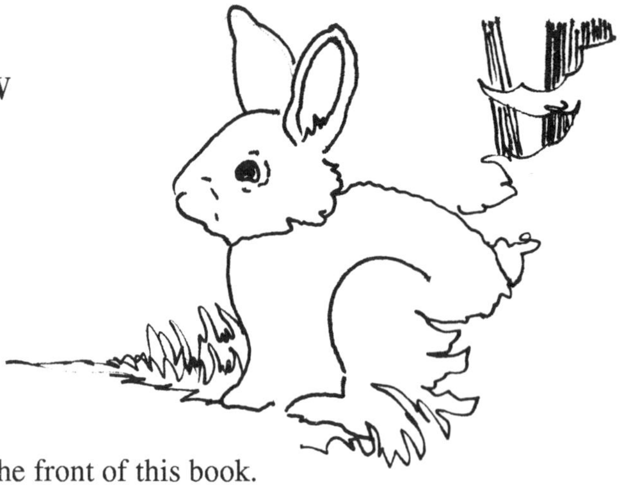

## FRESH SNOW

**PAPER SIZE:** 11" x 15"

**PALETTE**

Ultramarine Blue
New Gamboge
Winsor Blue
Winsor Violet
Burnt Sienna
Cobalt Blue
Burnt Umber

Transfer the pattern following the directions at the front of this book.

Mask out the clumps of snow on the branches of the trees using masking fluid. If you've never used masking fluid before there are directions on how to use it at the front of this book. Masking fluid protects the paper so that you may paint, then remove the masking fluid and have clean, white paper underneath.

**SKY**

Mix medium value gray blue (Ultramarine Blue + Burnt Sienna). Wet the sky area, from the horizon line up to the top of the paper. Look for a nice, even shine. Pick up a small amount of gray blue mix in the 8 round brush. Tilt the handle of the brush over so that you'll be using more of the side, rather than the tip. Stroke right at the top edge of the paper. Lift the brush and make another stroke (or even two) underneath. That will be enough for this tiny sky area. Now here's the difficult part...just let the color soften out as it wishes.

While this is drying, mix a medium value rust (Brown Madder + Burnt Umber).

**BACKGROUND TREES**

After the sky is completely dry, carefully rewet from the horizon up. Stroke lightly so that the sky color won't dislodge. Once again, look for that shine. Pick up a small amount of the rust mix (Brown Madder + Burnt Umber) in the tip of the 8 round brush. As before, use the side of the brush rather than just the tip. This will give you a "softer" look. Set the brush down at the TOP of the tree line and pull downward, filling in the entire tree line. Keep this color rather light. Rinse the brush, dry it, and fan it out. Then pick up one drop of the sky color (Ultramarine Blue + Burnt Sienna) and lightly stroke it over the rust, all across the tree line. Let this dry.

**WATER**

Mix medium value gray (Ultramarine Blue + Burnt Umber). Wet from the snowbank up to the bottom of the tree line. Do this carefully around the snowbanks. Remember, you are actually forming the top of the snow when you paint in that water behind it! So make that shape interesting...not just straight across.

Before you apply color, check to be sure that shine is there. Then set the brush down at the bottom and stroke it back and forth horizontally, working upward. The color should get gradually lighter as it reaches the tree line.

**TREE**

Mix these colors for the tree:

Medium Value Yellow Green (New Gamboge + Cobalt Blue)
Dark Value Blue Green (Winsor Blue + Burnt Umber)

Wet the tree and outward a good inch or so (to allow room for the tree to soften). As you apply the color pay special attention to the shape of the tree. Some branches stick way out. In other areas the color does not go outward as far. Use the 1 inch brush to float on medium value yellow green (New Gamboge + Cobalt Blue) over most of the tree. Then, take a look at it. You want to apply the dark value blue green (Winsor Blue + Burnt Umber) when the paper is still slightly shiny - but NOT PUDDLY! You want to darken the next application, but that will not happen if there's water puddling...all of that water will simply dilute the color! So, pick up the dark green with the 8 round brush and begin to put it onto the tree when there is just a slight shine. This color looks particularly nice directly under the snow clumps. And here's something fun you can try: sprinkle on a little salt. The salt must be put on while the paper is still wet. That is, not super shiny, but a bit of a shine. It will also work better if your board is at a bit of an incline. Just put your masking tape under one end. Salt will give you an interesting texture. Can you see it in the photo, at the top of my tree?

If you don't get enough color onto the tree the first time, you can rewet and apply more. The salt can only be used the first time around, though. If there's already a layer of paint underneath, it just won't be as effective. Let it dry thoroughly, paint on top of it, wipe it off with a damp paper towel, so as not to smudge if off onto the clean paper.

Put detail onto the tree with the dark value blue green (Winsor Blue + Burnt Umber) and your liner brush. On dry paper, draw on many needles. Start right up under the snow clumps and draw them outward.

## SNOW CLUMPS

All of these clumps must be shaded. Mix a medium value gray violet (Winsor Violet + touch of sky color), and a medium value Cobalt Blue. Paint each clump separately. Wet it first with clean water, then use the 8 round brush to stroke on one, or both, of the shading colors across the bottom. Rinse the brush, and soften the top edge of the color so that THE TOP OF THE SNOW CLUMP REMAINS CLEAN, WHITE PAPER!! Don't allow the shading to completely cover the snow or it will look dirty. If shading color goes too far, use a dry brush and a pressure stroke to push back the paint. Or you can simply blot hard, and redo it. When they're dry, paint in a few limbs and branches with dark value Burnt Umber. You may also wish to pull a few needles out of the clumps.

## OTHER SNOW

All of the rest of the snow along the bottom of the painting is done with the same shading colors as the clumps. There are some lines given for you on the pattern. Each line is a different snowbank. Do each snowbank separately. Wet above the line, and float the shading color on at the bottom of the wet area, right up next to the line of clean, white paper. Then rinse the brush and soften the top edge of color. Just as with the clumps of snow on the tree, the snowbanks should be white at the top. When they are dry, you may rewet a few places and dab on a small bit of the dark value blue green (Winsor Blue + Burnt Umber). This will be a base for grass. When it's dry, use a liner brush to pull up blades of grass out of the dark, soft color.

## BUNNY

This little bunny is fun and easy. Mix a medium value Burnt Umber. Carefully base in his little head with this mixture - leave white on his muzzle area, and the inside of the ear. It's also a bit lighter right around the eye. When dry, also base in his body with this color. While this is drying, thicken the Burnt Umber by adding a bit more color. Then wet his back as well as out into the tree a bit with clean water. Darken this mix just to the front of his hind leg and up onto his back - because the paper is wet there, it will soften slightly. His back should be rather fuzzy looking. Dry all of this thoroughly.

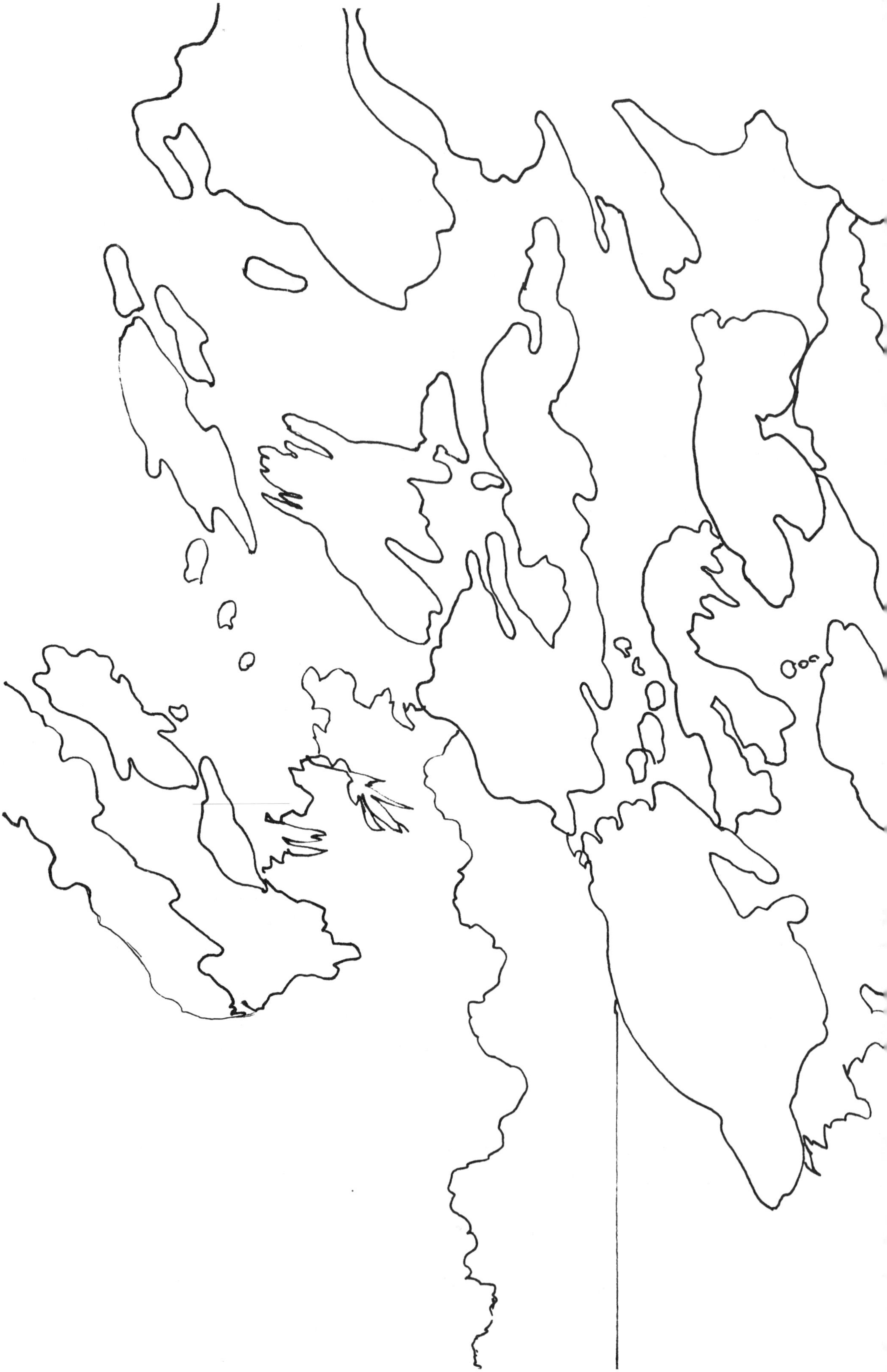

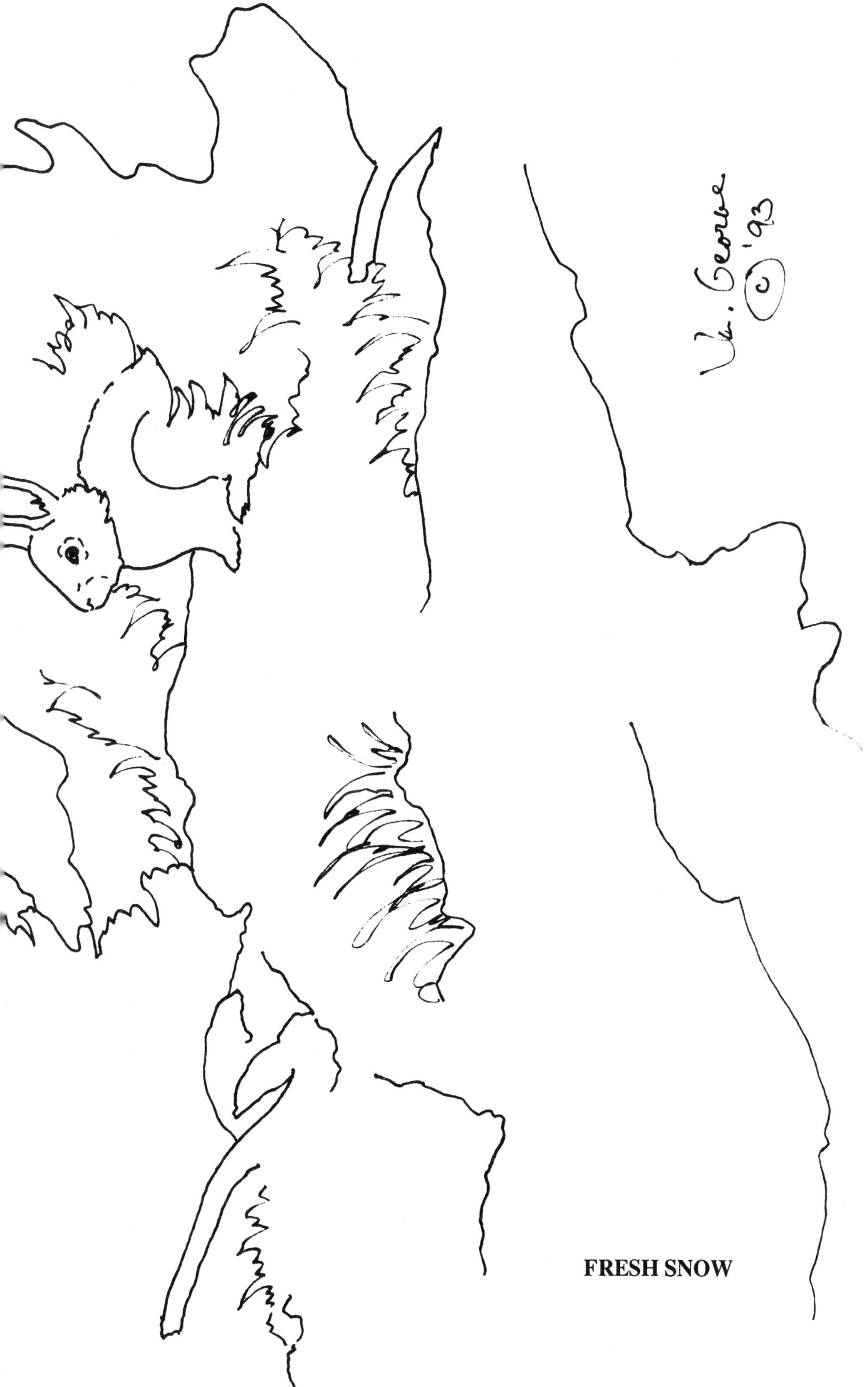

FRESH SNOW

Now, use the liner brush and medium value Burnt Umber to give him fur. The most important thing to remember here is to "contour" your strokes. That is, make your brush go in the same direction that his hair grows. You could also pretend that you are petting him, and that is the same direction that you would paint on the tiny hairs. Don't try to make him really dark the first time around. He will look much softer if you apply two coats instead. Paint the eye with Burnt Umber + touch of Ultramarine Blue. Finally, try painting on a few tiny hairs of acrylic White, or gesso. Don't forget you'll have to thin it a little. This works great if your fur has gotten really dark.

**FINALLY:**

Darken the entire right corner of the painting by wetting it with clean water and stroking on more shadow color. That color is:

Dark Value Gray Violet (Winsor Violet + touch of sky color)

You may also spatter there with the dark value blue green (Winsor Blue + Burnt Umber). If you've never spattered before you may want to cover up the top half of the painting! There are some great tips on spattering in the front of this book.

Pull some branches and twigs out to the snow with dark value Burnt Umber + touch of Ultramarine Blue. Then put a small shadow under the bunny with medium value gray (Ultramarine Blue + Burnt Sienna). Just paint it onto dry paper.

**Matting Suggestions:** Outside - Crescent 3297, Inside - Crescent 977

## CAT IN THE GARDEN

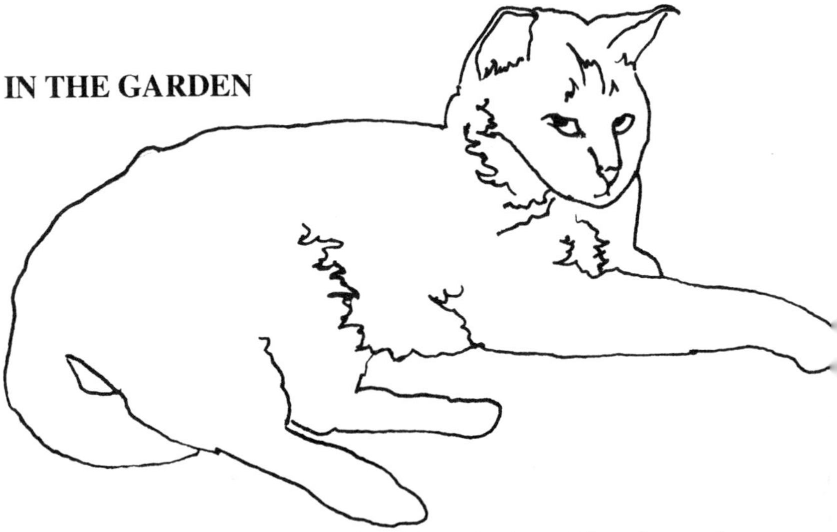

**PAPER SIZE:** 15" x 22"

**PALETTE**

| | |
|---|---|
| Winsor Blue | Viridian |
| Brown Madder | Burnt Sienna |
| Cobalt Blue | Alizarin Crimson |
| New Gamboge | Payne's Gray |
| Burnt Sienna | Winsor Violet |
| Raw Sienna | |

My next door neighbor's big, fat white cat was the inspiration for this painting. They have the biggest cats here in Ohio, and this one is so smug. He thinks everyone's garden belongs to him.

Transfer the pattern onto the paper following the instructions at the front of this book. All of the flowers and leaves appear on the pattern just as they were painted, but if you have done a few watercolors before you may wish to transfer only the flowers and try placing your own leaves! It's fun, and I'll tell you exactly what to do.

**BACKGROUND**

You will begin with the green background area behind the flowers and the cat. This is actually more than a simple background, it is a base upon which you will build the flowers and leaves. After this first step, the background will not yet be as dark as it appears in the finshed painting.

Mix: the folowing:
Medium Value Cobalt Blue
Medium Value Teal (Viridian + Winsor Blue + Brown Madder)

Start by wetting the entire left side of the paper, being careful not to get any water onto the cat. Make sure the paper is evenly wet - no puddles and no dry spots. The paper must be SHINY! If at any time the paper loses it's shine, you must stop. It is much better to completely dry the paper, rewet it, and then continue to paint.

Using the 1" flat brush, pick up the medium value Cobalt Blue. Simply set the brush down here and there. It's a sort of "X" motion, like feather-dusting, but slower. DO NOT BLEND! The very best background will have some holes in the color and look very mottled. The color is strongest along the bottom left and fades out as it moves up and outward. So, set your brush down first where the color is the strongest and then just "clean your brush" out as you stroke up and outward. After a bit of the Cobalt Blue, pick up the green and do the same. It's alright to get some of the color on the flowers. Flip-flop it onto the still shiny paper. You will be able to see individual brush strokes, and that's great! Just what you want. So, resist the temptation to "fix" anything because it will only blend and muddy your color. Trust me! Let this dry thoroughly. You're background should be a soft color, not too dark, and in some places the white paper may still show through.

**FLOWERS**

Mix a light value Alizarin Crimson. If you study the photo you will notice that some of the flowers are more detailed than others. Those flowers in front of another flower, or closest to the cat are the most detailed. These are petunias which can be separated into two sections - the large, flat surface, and the long funnel-shaped section. Keep in mind that the color values of the funnel section and the flat section will have to be different if you are going to paint the form correctly. That simply means if the funnel section and the flat section will have to be different if you are going to paint the form correctly. That simply means if the funnel is dark, the flat section should be light or visa versa. Try one. Paint the funnel section in lightly with the Alizarin Crimson mix. Let it dry, then study the flat section. Hmmmm. The funnel is dark. That means the front of the flat sections must remain light to separate it. But it should have some color, right? So, wet the back half and touch your color into the center and allow it to float out, but not all of the way to the front. Try another. This time leave the funnel light, and paint the entire flat section darker with Alizarin Crimson. Got the hang of it?

**LEAVES**

You will use negative painting to create the leaves. If you are new to watercolor, remember it's perfectly all right for you to paint the leaves on just as they are shown on the pattern. That's what they're there for. However, if you've been at this for a little while, I hope you'll give negative painting a chance. It opens up entire new worlds in watercolor!! Ready?

Let your background work for you. Look for a light spot, or a line made by a brush stroke. This could be a leaf...not the dark spots, rather a LIGHT area. It will help to pencil leaves in as you find them. After you "find" a few, begin to paint. Once you get into this, you'll get better and better at it. Think of the background now as a sort of jigsaw puzzle. The flowers are pieces, the leaves are pieces, and the spaces BETWEEN the leaves and flowers are also pieces. It's these in between spaces that you'll be painting. That's negative painting! Mix a medium value grayed teal (Winsor Blue + Burnt Sienna). Begin to fill in between some of your leaves with this color. Soon you will see them begin to appear. Keep in mind that the color gets lighter as you move up and outward from the corner. Therefore, when you get up to the level of the cat's back, begin to prewet the in-between spaces with clean water. Then, touch the color up next to the leaf, rinse the brush, and soften it out to nothing. No hard edges of color in the background. Remember, you want it to appear as all of this was done in one step, not be obvious that you painted around all of the leaves!

Mix: the following:

Light Value Yellow Green (New Gamboge + Payne's Gray)

Medium Value Blue Green (Ultramarine Blue + New Gamboge + a touch of Burnt Sienna)

Well, you're finished with the hard part! All that's left now is to paint a bit of color onto the leaves. Not all of them are painted. Some remain just as they are, others receive only a simple vein line. To do that, wet one side of the leaf only with the 4 round brush. Pick up one drop of a green in the tip of the brush and dab it onto the wet side, right next to the vein line. Quickly, rinse the brush, fan it out a bit and blend so that the color fades as it moves away from the vein line. Easy, huh? Continue painting leaves, use different greens, do one side of some leaves, both sides of others.

**CAT**

Because this cat is white, the only parts of him that are painted are the parts in shadow. Begin by forming his right side by negative painting. Wet the background behind him there and float on medium value teal (Viridian + Winsor Blue + Brown Madder) right up next to him. Rinse the brush and soften out to the right. Then mix these other shading colors:

Light Value Cobalt Blue
Light Value Winsor Violet
Medium Value Navy Blue (Winsor Blue + Brown Madder)

Begin on the face. Pick up a bit of light value Cobalt Blue in the tip of the 8 round brush and shade the length of the nose. Quickly, rinse the brush and soften the right edge of color. Using this same mix, continue to shade the cheek, the chin, side of the face and just to the right of the ear. Study the photo now to familiarize yourself with the shading on his body. It is a mix of both Cobalt Blue and

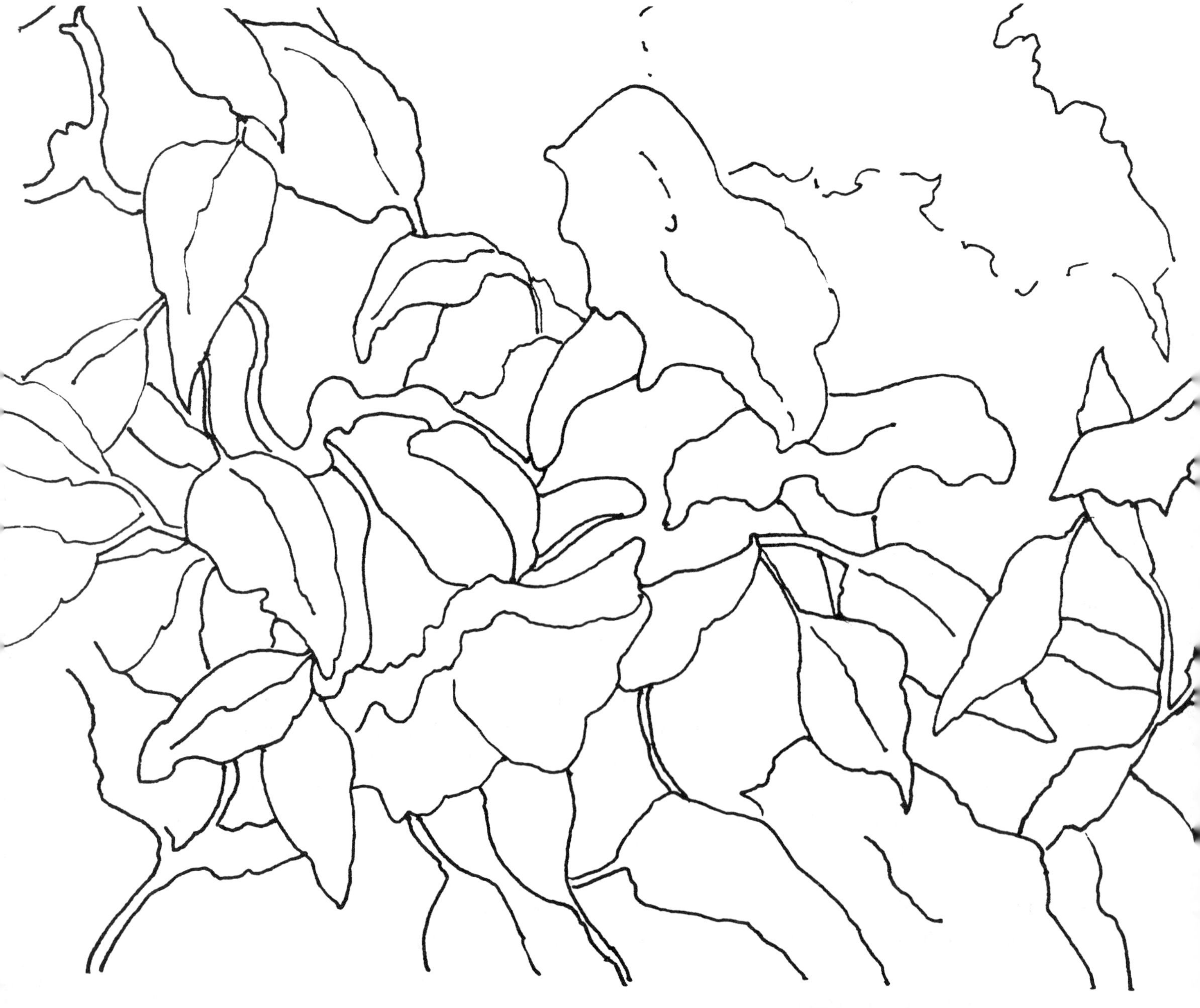

the Winsor Violet mixes - paint one mix onto the cat with short "pulling" strokes to give the feeling of fur. Then, pick up the other color and paint short pulling strokes, letting the two colors mix while they're wet. The medium value navy blue (Winsor Blue + Brown Madder) is used to darken the body where he sits down into the flowers. A bit of light value Raw Sienna was also used just at the back of the shoulder blade. 

**EARS AND EYES**

Prewet the inside of the ear with light value Raw Sienna, and while still wet dab on one drop of Alizarin Crimson right at the base. Leave a thin line of dry, white paper to separate the inside and outside of his ear. Wet the outside of the ear with light value Alizarin Crimson, and while wet dab on one drop of the navy blue mix (Winsor Blue + Brown Madder). The other ear is simply painted with light value Alizarin Crimson.

Wet the eye carefully with light value Raw Sienna. While it is still wet, pick up a bit of medium value Burnt Sienna in the liner brush and carefully draw along the outside edge of the eye letting the color flow softly inward. This Burnt Sienna should not take over the yellow of the eye completely. If it does, blot it out quickly with a paper towel and try again. When dry, paint the pupil with a dark value navy blue (Winsor Blue + Brown Madder).

The nose is prewet with clean water, then Alizarin Crimson is touched just at the bottom. Soften any hard lines of color, and when it's dry paint in the nostril with the navy blue mix used on the pupil. There! Isn't he cute...and fat?

**PILLOW**

All of the squares of the pillow are painted with medium value Cobalt Blue, but add more water and get lighter as you paint to the right side of the pillow. Those sections that are right under the cat should be rewet, and shaded with a touch of dark value navy blue (Winsor Blue + Brown Madder).

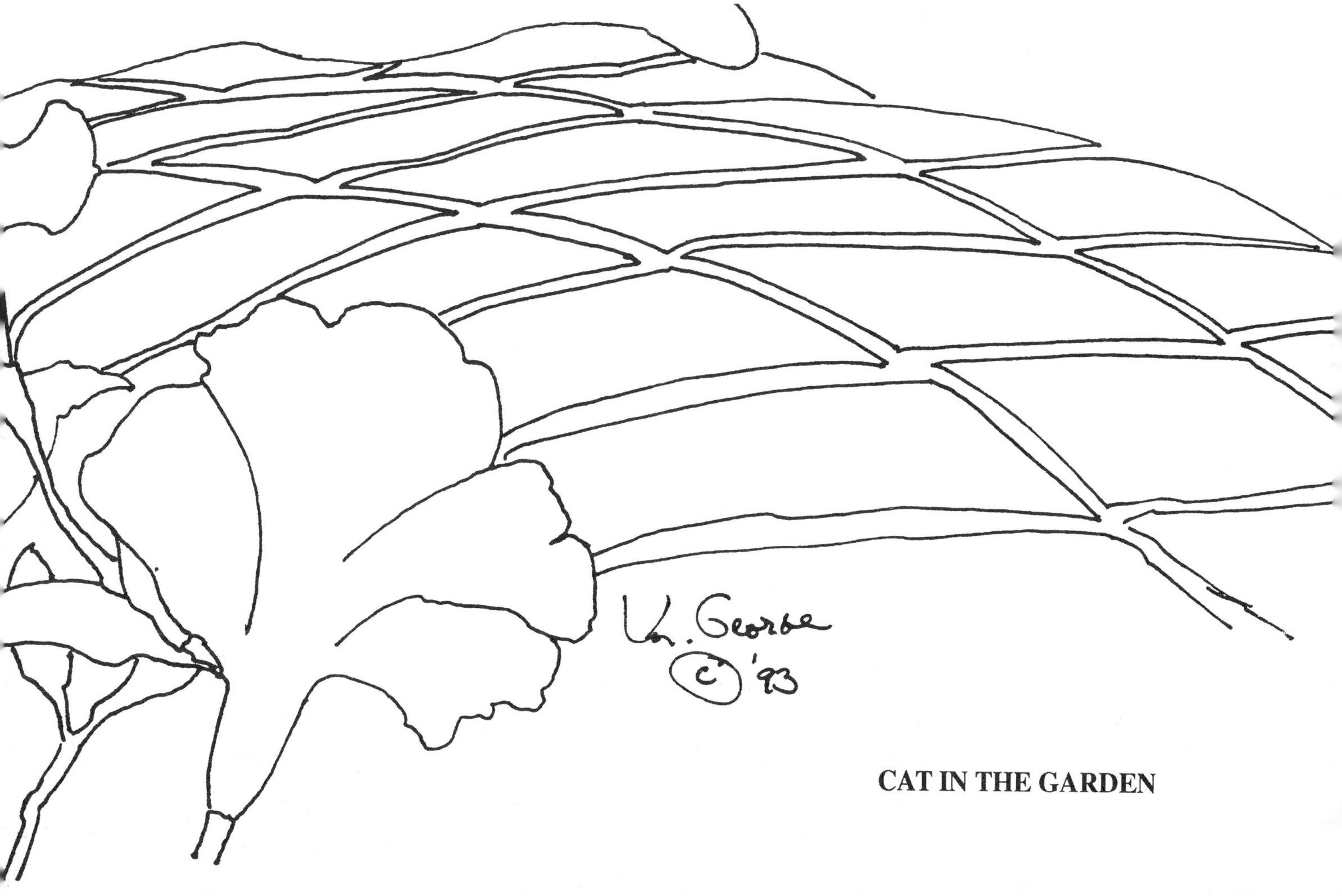


**CAT IN THE GARDEN**

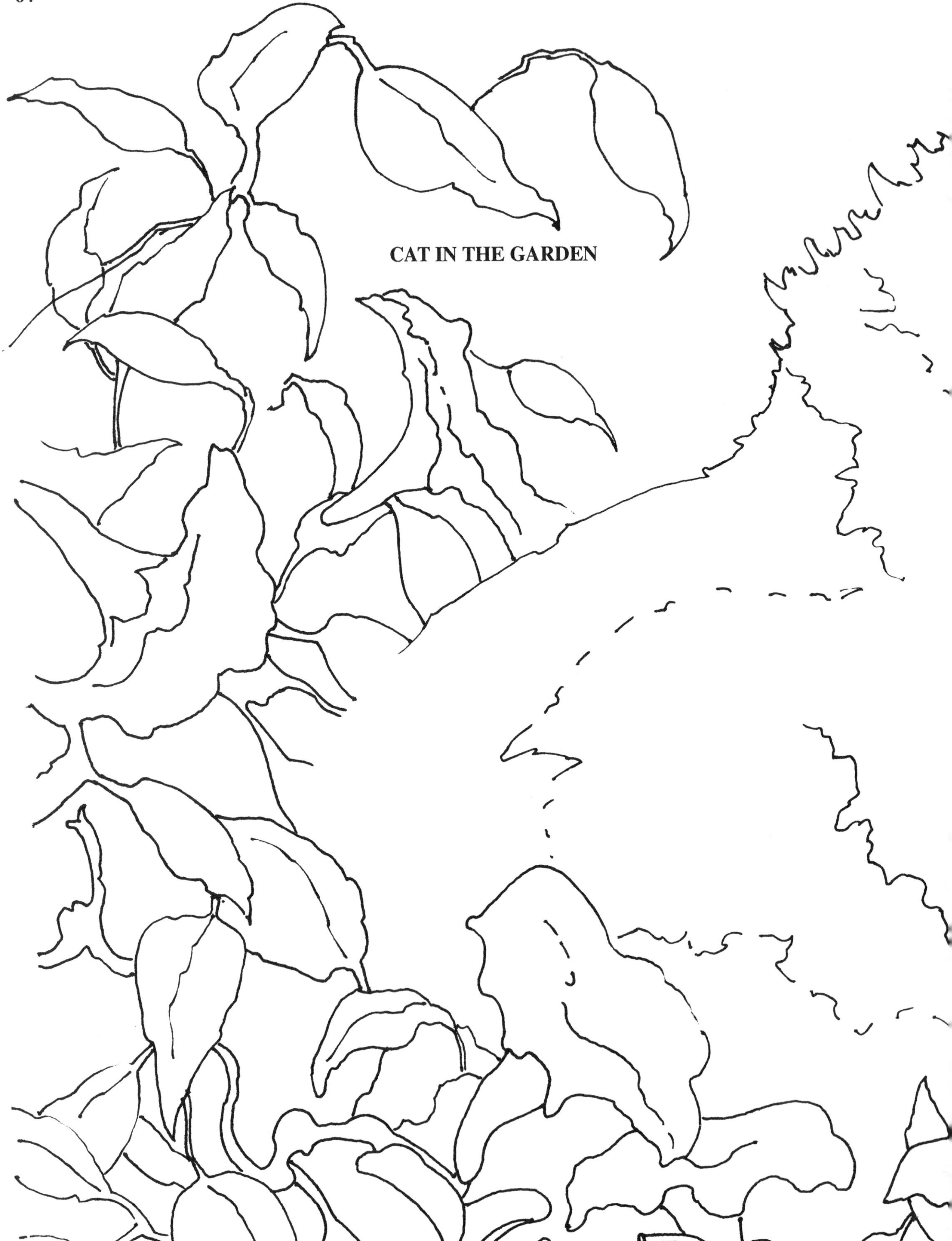
CAT IN THE GARDEN

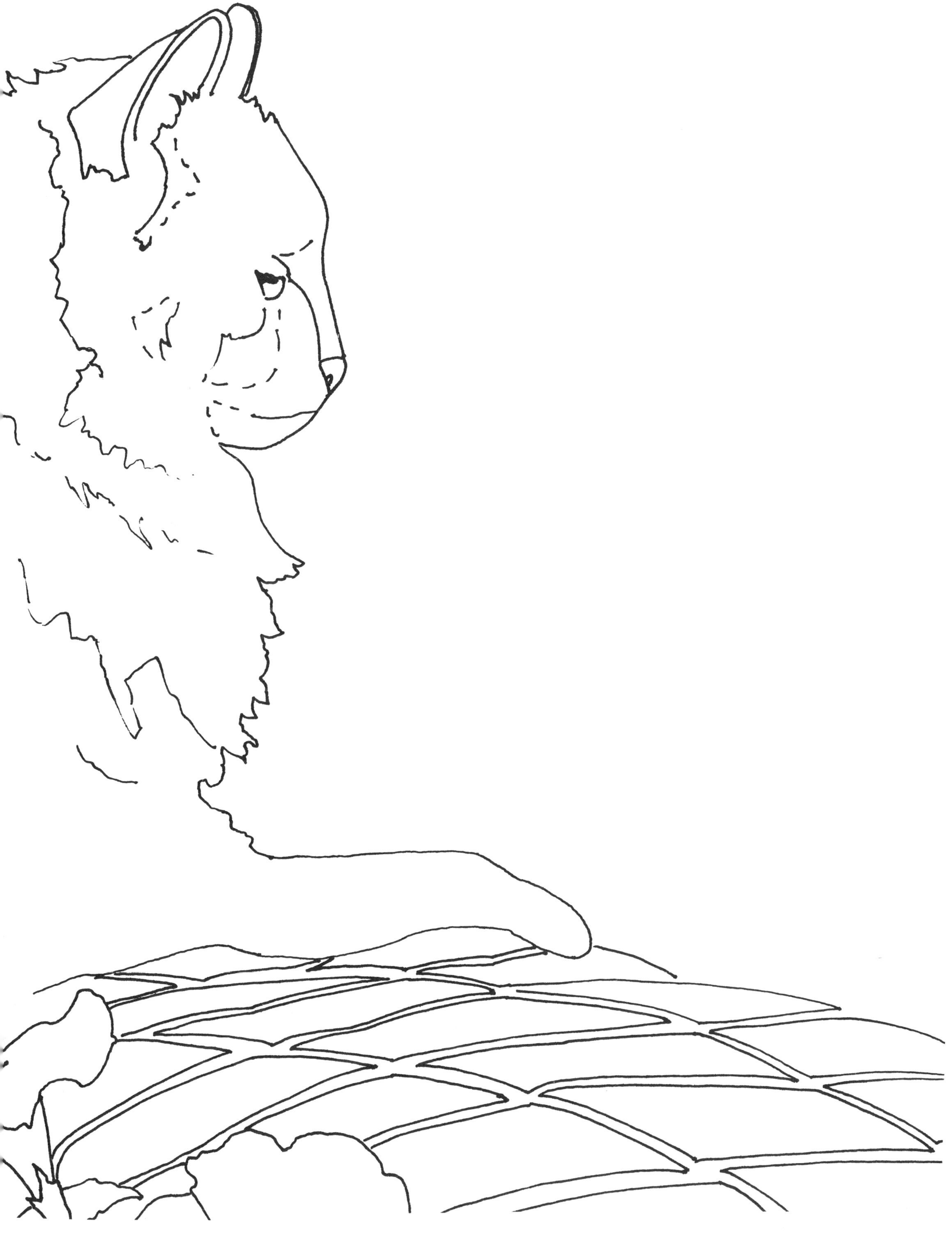

# TEA TIME

**PAPER SIZE:** 15" x 15"

**PALETTE**

| | |
|---|---|
| Cobalt Blue | Burnt Umber |
| Alizarin Crimson | Cadmium Red |
| Brown Madder | Raw Sienna |
| Neutral Tint | New Gamboge |
| Payne's Gray | Cadmium Orange |
| Ultramarine Blue | |

Transfer the pattern following the instructions at the front of this book.

## STRAWBERRY ICE CREAM IN GLASS

Mix light value Alizarin Crimson, and a medium value pink (Alizarin Crimson + Cadmium Red).

Base in the ice cream with light value Alizarin Crimson, and while it's still wet dab on bits of medium value pink to shade. There is a large area near the bottom of the ice cream that remains very pale. That is where the ice cream is touching the glass. Let it dry, then begin the glass. Mix a light value blue (Cobalt Blue + a touch of Burnt Umber). Working on dry paper paint the glass except for the reflections and markings given for you on the pattern. Yes, you paint right over the ice cream where the front portion of the glass crosses over it. There is also a line of clean, white paper that remains all along the front rim. At this point, you're ready to paint in the markings of the bowl of the glass, and shade the stem. Darken your original blue mix just a bit (Cobalt Blue + Burnt Umber). The markings are little circles that are stacked up several in a row. But what you paint are simply the bottoms of those little circles - you paint little U-shapes that fit into the bottom of each little circle. Just paint them onto dry paper, and don't worry about blending, they're too little! Also, shade a little bit extra along the bottom of the bowl of the glass, over ice cream and all. Then study the photo to help you with placement of the shading on the stem. These shapes are also given for you on the pattern. Simply fill them in on dry paper.

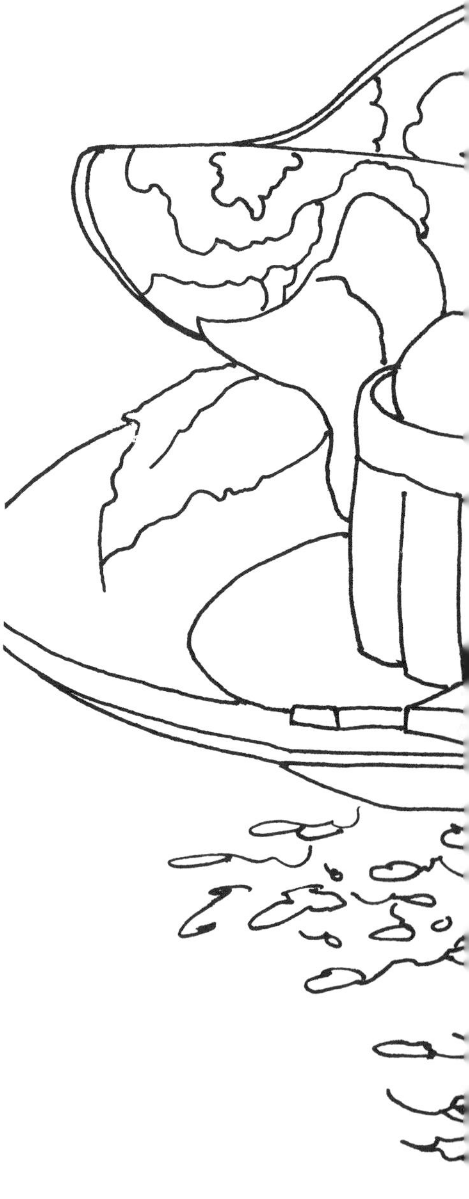

## STRAWBERRIES

Begin the strawberries by basing them with a medium value of Alizarin Crimson. While the basecoat is still wet, dab on the medium value pink (Alizarin Crimson + Cadmium Red) to shade. Brown Madder was also used to shade the berries in the ceramic container. After they're dry, light spots of Alizarin Crimson were gently placed in rows with the tip of the 4 round brush to indicate the places where the seeds are.

## NAPKINS

Mix the following:

Medium Value Rose (Alizarin Crimson + Brown Madder)

**TEA TIME**

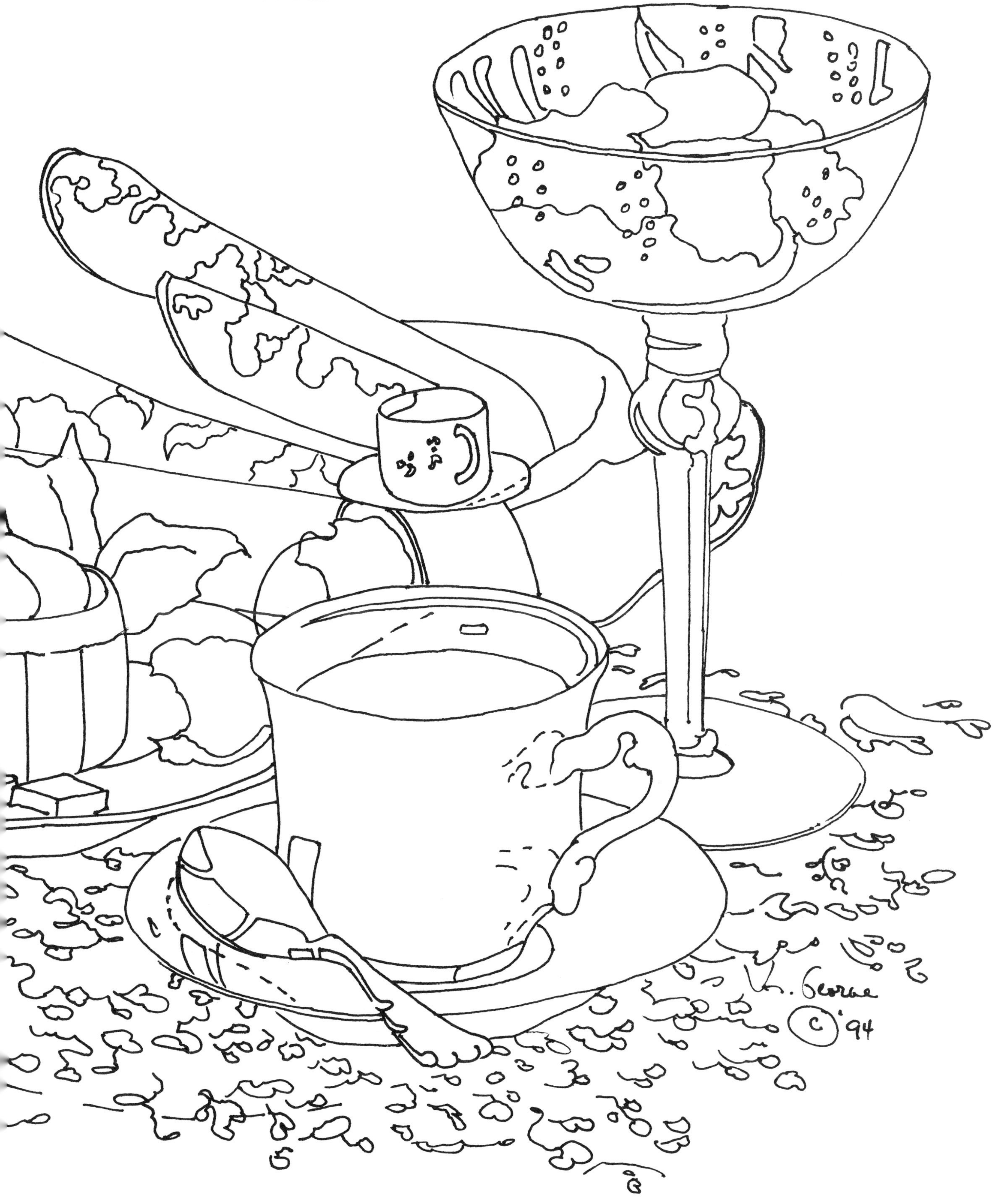

Medium Value Green (Winsor Blue + Burnt Umber)

Medium Value Blue Green (Above mix + more Winsor Blue)

Also, use the light value Alizarin Crimson mix from the ice cream. These napkins are covered with roses and leaves. I have laid out some of them for you on the pattern, but feel frees to add your own, or change them in any way you wish. All of the roses are based with the light value Alizarin Crimson and shaded with medium value rose (Alizarin Crimson + Brown Madder.) The shading is simply painted onto dry paper. However, you certainly could blend and soften it if you wish! The leaves are combinations of the two green mixes. Remember, the cooler the color, the further back in the painting it will seem. Therefore, where two folds cross, the leaves in the back could be the blue green mix, and the leaves on the front fold would be medium value green. The piping on the edges of the napkins is the rose mixture. When all of the flowers and leaves have been based in, you may find that some of the folds still need to be "separated". Try this: wash over any section you want to push back with a light value Cobalt Blue. (Remember, the cooler the color the further back in the painting it will seem). Repeat that wash as many times as necessary. Another tip would be to keep the color on the front fold darker than that of those folds in the back.

## TEA

These are the mixes for the tea: Medium Value Raw Sienna

Medium Value Burnt Sienna

Medium Value Burnt Umber

Medium Value Gray Brown (Burnt Umber + Neutral Tint)

The tea is a very golden color, until it reaches 1/3 of the way from the left, where it turns more gray-brown. Base in the right two-thirds of the tea with the Raw Sienna mix. Look for a shine! While this area is still shiny, dab the Burnt Sienna onto the right side and as you move into the middle, dab Burnt Umber. Finally, while all of this is still shiny wet, pick up the gray brown mix and base in the remaining one-third of the tea. Usually, it is best to allow all of these colors to soften as they wish, rather,than blend. If you must blend, remember to STOP BLENDING BEFORE THE PAPER LOSES THE SHINE. If you continue to blend past that point, each time you touch the brush to the paper it will pick up paint and make a streak. So, you're actually making things worse! If you find that the tea is not dark enough, simply wait for the area to dry completely, then rewet with clean water and reapply the color mixes just as you did the first time around. If you find that the tea is too dark, call it coffee! Ha!

## TEA CUP

Mix a medium value gray (Ultramarine Blue + Burnt Umber). Begin with the back rim of the cup. Fill in the shaded area (don't forget to paint around the tiny highlight!) Then quickly rinse the brush and soften that left edge of the color. Because the front of the cup is a much larger area, you may wish to wet it first to give you a lot more blending time. Wet the entire front of the cup with clean water and check to be sure it is SHINY! Then begin to apply the color by picking up a bit of the gray in the tip of the #8 round brush. Set the brush down a little to the right of the left edge (NOT on the edge itself). This should be the darkest area, and the color should lighten as it moves to the right, finally ending about two-thirds of the way over. The outer edges of color must be softened. Rinse the brush, press out the excess water and fan out the bristles a bit. Then quickly, place the brush half on the shading color and half off of it to soften. While this dries, paint the shadow onto the handle. Wet it, then using a #4 round, stroke the gray mix onto the lower side of the handle. Carefully soften the top edge of the color so that the top of the handle remains completely white. When dry, paint the shadows that are cast from the handle onto the side of the cup. These are painted onto dry paper, but softened out to the left.

## TEA TIME

Finally, study the photo to understand exactly where the shading is placed on the saucer. Wet the right side of the saucer, from the spoon over, and float on medium value gray (Ultramarine Blue + Burnt Umber) so that it is darkest behind the handle of the cup and lightens as it comes forward. Note that the paper remains white directly around the base of the cup! Then, wet the left side of the saucer, again from the spoon over. Just above the spoon, the paper remains white, but is suddenly quite dark all along the left edge of the saucer. Place medium value Burnt Umber right up next to the left edge of the bowl of the spoon, then soften it out as it moves away from the spoon. Both the cup and the saucer have a rim of green that starts dark in one area, but fades slowly away to nothing. Use medium value green (Winsor Blue + Burnt Umber) and a liner brush to carefully line the rim. Set your brush down where the color is the darkest, then pick up clean water in the brush and continue along the rim fading the color as you go.

### SPOON

Base the spoon with light value Raw Sienna, keeping the bowl of the spoon quite a bit lighter than the handle. When dry, shade the spoon with the gray brown mix (Burnt Umber + Neutral Tint). Simply fill in the shadow areas on dry paper.

### CERAMIC

The ceramic is based with light value Raw Sienna, and while wet a bit of medium value Burnt Sienna is dabbed here and there. If you take a look at the photo you will notice that the ceramic is divided into section - each is primarily brown, except for a small pink area at the top. The small sections are formed by wetting each separately, then dabbing a bit of Burnt Sienna on the bottom left edge of the section. At the top, medium value Alizarin Crimson + Cadmium Red was used instead. The saucer below the ceramic is shaded with medium value gray (Winsor Blue + Brown Madder). Paint it on by pre-wetting with clean water, floating on the shading, then rinse the brush and soften if need be. Study the photo and pattern to place the shading.

### LEAVES

Mix the following two greens. They are both mixed from the same colors, but one simply has more Payne's Gray than the other:

Medium Value Yellow Green (New Gamboge + Payne's Gray)

Medium Value Green (New Gamboge + more Payne's Gray)

These leaves are nothing fancy. They can be filled in on dry paper, or for a bit more detail, wet one half of the leaf at a time and dab on color allowing it to float out as it wishes. The one important thing about these leaves is to be sure that their color is more yellow green than the leaves in the napkins. Otherwise it will all blend together!

### STARFRUIT

I know, this looks like butter. Well, it's really pieces of starfruit. Starfruit has definite edges and corners, just like butter. To make it look right there must be a definite value change from the light side to the dark side. The light sides of the fruit are painted with a light value of Cadmium Orange. The dark sides are filled in with a medium value Cadmium Orange and then shaded with Brown Madder + touch of Alizarin Crimson, dabbed onto the still wet orange base color. Rinse the brush and soften out any hard lines of shading color.

### TABLECLOTH

Now, you're almost finished! The tablecloth is one of those subjects that looks really hard, but

## TEA TIME

really is easy. Mix a medium value violet gray (Cobalt Blue + Alizarin Crimson). The very easiest way to go about the tablecloth is to trace off all of the little designs from the pattern, and then simply fill them is with this color. Use whatever brush you feel comfortable with and don't worry if you end up making the designs a little different. It really doesn't matter at all!!

Finally, paint soft shadows onto the tablecloth. These shadows are cast from the cup and saucers. Use medium value gray (Ultramarine Blue + Burnt Umber). You may wish to wet the shadow really is easy. Mix a medium value violet gray (Cobalt Blue + Alizarin Crimson). The very easiest way to go about the tablecloth is to trace off all of the little designs from the pattern and then simply fill them in with this color. Use whatever brush you feel comfortable with, and don't worry if you end up area first to give you more blending time. Remember that the shadows will be darkest right next to the object that is casting them, so set your brush down there. Then quickly work outward gradually getting lighter and lighter.

**MATTING SUGGESTIONS:** Outside, Crescent 3300 - Inside, Crescent 908

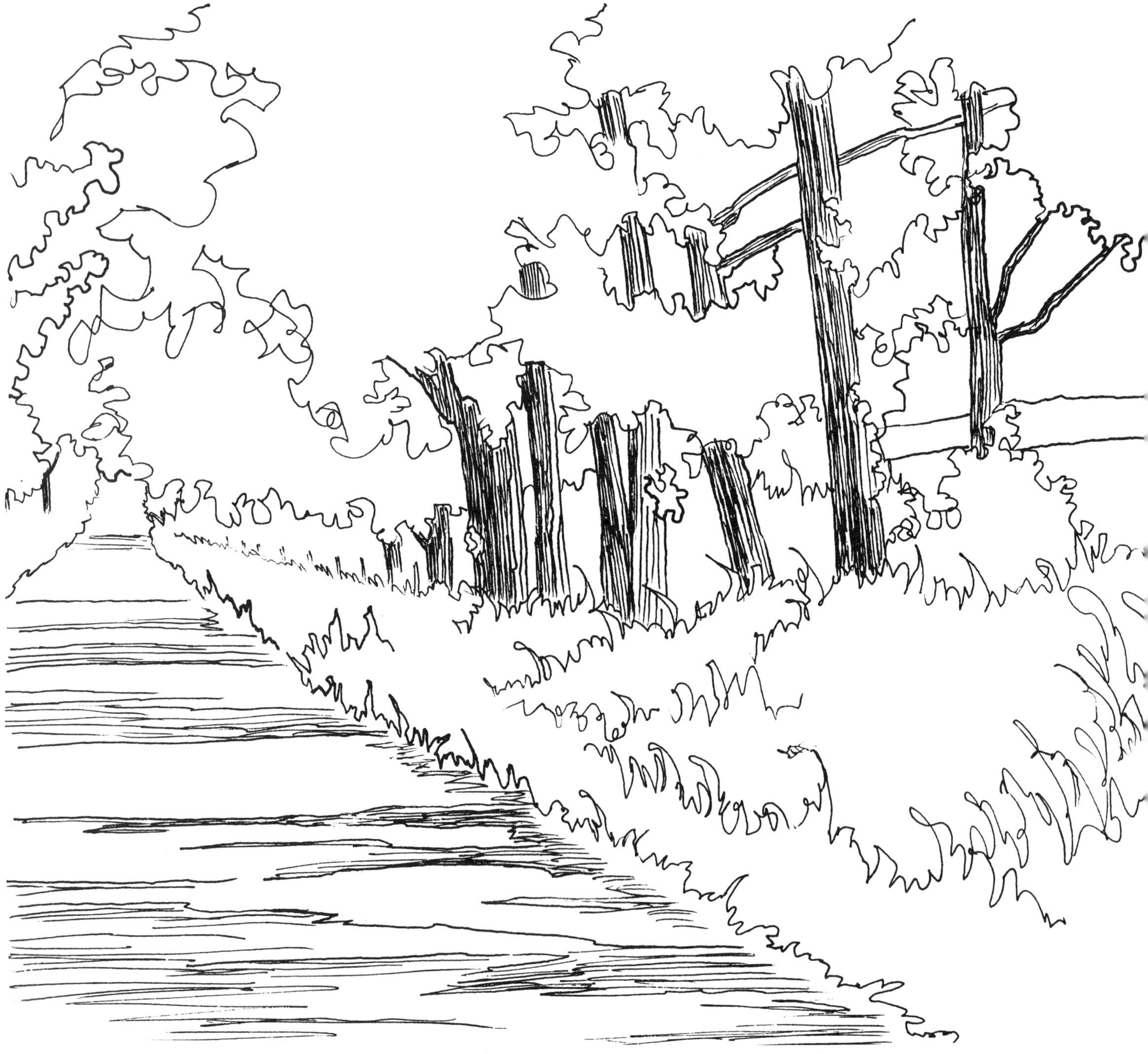

## OIL BOOKS

| Vol. | Title | No. | Price |
|---|---|---|---|
| ol.1 | "His and Hers" by Susan Scheewe | 101 | $6.50 |
| ol. 5 | "So Dear To My Heart" by Susan Scheewe | 105 | $5.50 |
| ol. 6 | "Brushed With Elegance" by Susan Scheewe | 106 | $5.50 |
| ol. 7 | "Paint 'n Patch" by Susan Scheewe | 107 | $5.50 |
| ol. 11 | "I Love To Paint" by Susan Scheewe | 111 | $6.50 |
| ol. 14 | "Enjoy Painting Animals" by Susan Scheewe | 114 | $6.50 |
| ol. 17 | "Countryside Reflections" by Susan Scheewe | 161 | $6.50 |
| ol. 18 | "Mostly Landscapes" by Susan Scheewe | 216 | $8.50 |
| ol. 19 | "Gift of Painting" by Susan Scheewe...O/AC/WC | 230 | $8.50 |
| ol. 1 | "Western Images" by Becky Anthony | 186 | $6.50 |
| ol. 3 | "Fantasy Flowers II" by Georgia Bartlett | 129 | $6.50 |
| ol. 4 | "Soft Petals" by Georgia Bartlett | 171 | $6.50 |
| ol. 6 | "Painting Fantasy Flowers" by Georgia Bartlett | 215 | $7.50 |
| ol. 7 | "Flowers" by Georgia Bartlett *NEW** | 290 | $8.50 |
| ol. 1 | "Painting, A Barrel of Fun" by Donna Bell | 194 | $6.50 |
| ol. 2 | "Painting, A Barrel of Fun" by Donna Bell | 201 | $7.50 |
| ol. 3 | "Barnscapes and More" by Donna Bell | 218 | $8.50 |
| ol. 4 | "Countryscapes" by Donna Bell | 249 | $8.50 |
| ol. 5 | "Painter to Painter" by Donna Bell | 263 | $8.50 |
| ol. 6 | "Landscapes With Acrylics & Oil by Donna Bell *NEW** | 282 | $8.50 |
| ol. 1 | "Natures Palette" by Carol Binford.....O/AC | 248 | $8.50 |
| ol. 1 | "Oil Painting The Easy Way" by Bill Blackman | 219 | $8.50 |
| ol. 1 | "Mini Mini More" by Terri and Nancy Brown | 150 | $6.50 |
| ol. 2 | "Mini Mini More" by Terri and Nancy Brown | 151 | $6.50 |
| ol. 4 | "Heritage Trails" by Terri and Nancy Brown | 169 | $6.50 |
| ol. 6 | "Garden Trails" by Terri and Nancy Brown *NEW** | 283 | $8.50 |
| ol. 1 | "Windows of My World" by Jackie Clafin | 174 | $6.50 |
| ol. 2 | "Windows of My World" by Jackie Clafin | 181 | $7.50 |
| ol. 3 | "I'm Partial To Flowers" by Ellie Cook | 157 | $6.50 |
| ol. 1 | "Expressions In Oil" by Delores Egger | 154 | $6.50 |
| ol. 4 | "Expressions In Oil" by Delores Egger | 239 | $7.50 |
| ol. 1 | "Victorian Days" by Gloria Gaffney | 240 | $8.50 |
| Vol. 2 | "Days of Heaven" by Gloria Gaffney | 252 | $8.50 |
| Vol. 3 | "Winter Song" by Gloria Gaffney | 271 | $8.50 |
| Vol. 1 | "Roses Are For Everyone" by Bill Huffaker | 145 | $7.50 |
| Vol. 3 | "Nature's Beauty" by Bill Huffaker | 177 | $6.50 |
| Vol. 1 | "Copper, Silver, Brass and Glass" by Susan Jenkins | 211 | $6.50 |
| Vol. 1 | "Backroads of My Memory" by Geri Kisner | 225 | $7.50 |
| Vol. 2 | "Backroads of My Memory" by Geri Kisner | 245 | $7.50 |
| Vol. 1 | "Country's Edge" by Shirley Koenig....O/AC | 179 | $7.50 |
| Vol. 2 | "Country's Edge" by Shirley Koenig....O/AC | 212 | $6.50 |
| Vol. 3 | "Country's Edge" by Shirley Koenig....O/AC *NEW** | 291 | $8.50 |
| Vol. 1 | "Ducks and Geese" by Jean Lyles | 172 | $6.50 |
| Vol. 1 | "Pathway To Painting" by Lee McGowen *NEW** | 281 | $8.50 |
| Vol. 1 | "Stepping Stones" by Judy Nutter | 121 | $6.50 |
| Vol. 1 | "Rustic Charms" by Sharon Rachal | 175 | $6.50 |
| Vol. 2 | "Rustic Charms II" by Sharon Rachal | 199 | $7.50 |
| Vol. 3 | "Rustic Charms III" by Sharon Rachal | 217 | $6.50 |
| Vol. 4 | "Rustic Charms IV" by Sharon Rachal | 238 | $7.50 |
| Vol. 5 | "Rustic Charms V, Florals" by Sharon Rachal | 261 | $8.50 |
| Vol. 1 | "Painting Flowers With Augie" by Augie Reis | 152 | $6.50 |
| Vol. 1 | "Realistic Florals and More" by Judy Sleight | 233 | $8.50 |
| Vol. 2 | "Painting Realism" by Judy Sleight | 272 | $8.50 |
| Vol. 1 | "Soft & Misty Paintings" by Kathy Snider | 204 | $8.50 |
| Vol. 2 | "Soft & Misty Paintings" by Kathy Snider | 229 | $8.50 |
| Vol. 3 | "Soft & Misty Paintings" by Kathy Snider | 251 | $8.50 |
| Vol. 2 | "More Old Friends" by Gene Waggoner | 148 | $6.50 |
| Vol. 4 | "Friends We've Known" by Gene Waggoner | 187 | $7.50 |
| Vol. 5 | "Friends Are Forever" by Gene Waggoner | 231 | $7.50 |
| Vol. 1 | "Fantasy Folk" by Don Weed | 123 | $6.50 |
| Vol. 2 | "Painting The Clowns by Don Weed | 124 | $6.50 |
| Vol. 1 | "Something Special For Everyone" by Mildred Yeiser | 158 | $6.50 |
| Vol. 2 | "Something Special For Everyone" by Mildred Yeiser | 178 | $6.50 |
| Vol. 4 | "Something Special For Everyone" by Mildred Yeiser | 235 | $7.50 |
| Vol. 5 | "Soft and Gentle Paintings" by Mildred Yeiser | 268 | $8.50 |

## FABRIC PAINTING BOOKS

| Vol. | Title | No. | Price |
|---|---|---|---|
| Vol. 1 | "Painting It's Our Bag" by Bev Hink/Susan Scheewe | 193 | $8.50 |
| Vol. 1 | "Whimsical Critters" by Lori Ohlson | 228 | $7.50 |
| Vol. 1 | "Oh Those Little Rascals" by Diane Permenter | 247 | $7.50 |
| Vol. 6 | "Angels In My Stocking" by Diane Richards | 254 | $7.50 |
| Vol. 1 | "Creations In Canvas and More" by Carol Spooner | 256 | $7.50 |
| Vol. 2 | "Garden Gate" by Jolene Thompson | 250 | $7.50 |
| Vol. 5 | "Count Your Blessings" by Chris Thornton | 213 | $8.50 |
| Vol. 6 | "Share Your Blessings" by Chris Thornton | 226 | $8.50 |
| Vol. 5 | "Daydreams and Sweet ShirtsII" by Don & Lynn Weed | 208 | $7.50 |
| Vol. 1 | "Floral Fabrics and Watercolor" by Sally Williams | 262 | $8.50 |

## PEN AND INK BOOKS / COLORED PENCIL BOOKS

| Vol. | Title | No. | Price |
|---|---|---|---|
| Vol. 2 | "Barnyards and Billygoats" by Claudia Nice | 134 | $6.50 |
| Vol. 3 | "Wing and Wildflowers" by Claudia Nice | 135 | $6.50 |
| Vol. 6 | "Journey of Memories" by Claudia Nice | 166 | $6.50 |
| Vol. 7 | "Scenes from Seasons Past" by Claudia Nice | 183 | $8.50 |
| Vol. 8 | "Taste of Summer" by Claudia Nice | 223 | $8.50 |
| *NEW** Vol. 9 | "Familiar Faces" by Claudia Nice | 284 | $8.50 |
| Vol. 1 | "Colored Pencil Made Easy" by Jane Wunder | 232 | $7.50 |
| Vol. 2 | "Colored Pencil Made Easy" by Jane Wunder | 242 | $7.50 |
| Vol. 3 | "The Beauty of Colored Pencil and Ink Drawing" by Jane Wunder | 259 | $7.50 |

## VIDEOS BY SUSAN SCHEEWE BROWN

|  |  |
|---|---|
| "The Gift of Painting Simply Watercolor" 60 minutes | $24.95 |
| "The Gift of Painting" 90 minutes | $24.95 |
| "Paintings For The Holidays" 60 minutes | $24.95 |
| "Watercolor & Oil Do Mix" 60 minutes | $24.95 |
| "Watercolor Special Effects" 60 minutes | $24.95 |
| "Fabric Painting Fun" 60 minutes | $24.95 |

*SUSAN SCHEEWE PUBLICATIONS*

*13435 N.E. WHITAKER WAY PORTLAND, OR. 97230*

*PH. (503) 254-9100 FAX (503) 252-9508*

# Susan Scheewe Publications Inc.

## ACRYLIC BOOKS

| | | | | |
|---|---|---|---|---|
| | Vol. 19 | "Gift of Painting" by Susan Scheewe....O/AC/WC | 230 | $8.50 _____ |
| | Vol. 1 | "Painting It's Our Bag" by Bev Hink/Susan Scheewe | 193 | $8.50 _____ |
| | Vol. 4 | "Keepsake Sampler" by Susan & Camille Scheewe | 200 | $6.50 _____ |
| | Vol. 1 | "Loving You" by Susan & Camille Scheewe | 244 | $7.50 _____ |
| NEW* | Vol. 1 | "Keepsakes For The Holidays" by Charleen Stempel & Susan Scheewe | 286 | $8.50 _____ |
| | Vol. 1 | "Kids and Water" by Joyce Benner | 234 | $8.50 _____ |
| | Vol. 1 | "Natures Palette" by Carol Binford | 248 | $8.50 _____ |
| | Vol. 1 | "Santas and Sams" by Bobi Dolara | 258 | $8.50 _____ |
| | Vol. 2 | "Vintage Peace" by Bobi Dolara | 270 | $8.50 _____ |
| | Vol. 1 | "Holiday Gathering" by Angie Hupp | 267 | $8.50 _____ |
| NEW* | Vol. 2 | "Holiday Gathering" by Angie Hupp | 292 | $8.50 _____ |
| | Vol. 1 | "Happy Heart, Happy Home" by Cathy Jones | 241 | $7.50 _____ |
| | Vol. 1 | "Festive Collectibles" by Deborha Kerr | 279 | $8.50 _____ |
| NEW* | Vol. 2 | "Serendipity Collectibles" by Deborha Kerr | 289 | $8.50 _____ |
| | Vol. 1 | "Country's Edge" by Shirley Koenig......O/AC | 179 | $7.50 _____ |
| | Vol. 2 | "Country's Edge" by Shirley Koenig......O/AC | 212 | $6.50 _____ |
| NEW* | Vol. 3 | "Country's Edge" by Shirley Koenig......O/AC | 291 | $8.50 _____ |
| | Vol. 1 | "Huckleberry Horse" by Hanna Long | 269 | $8.50 _____ |
| | Vol. 1 | "Love Lives Here" by Mary Lynn Lewis | 170 | $6.50 _____ |
| | Vol. 2 | "Love Lives Here" by Mary Lynn Lewis | 185 | $6.50 _____ |
| | Vol. 3 | "Love Lives Here" by Mary Lynn Lewis | 195 | $6.50 _____ |
| NEW* | Vol. 1 | "Special Welcomes" by Corinne Miller | 287 | $8.50 _____ |
| NEW* | Vol. 2 | "Special Welcomes" by Corinne Miller | 298 | $8.50_____ |
| | Vol 1 | "Fruit & Flower Fantasies" by Joyce Morrison | 277 | $8.50 _____ |
| | Vol. 1 | "Wildflower Sampler" by Bev Norman | 191 | $8.50 _____ |
| | Vol. 1 | "Whimsical Critters" by Lori Ohlson | 228 | $7.50 _____ |
| | Vol. 1 | "Holiday Medley" by Nina Owens | 265 | $8.50 _____ |
| NEW* | Vol. 2 | "Another Holiday Medley" by Nina Owens | 296 | $8.50 _____ |
| | Vol. 1 | "Oh Those Little Rascals" by Diane Permenter | 247 | $7.50 _____ |
| | Vol. 1 | "Forever In My Heart" by Diane Richards.....AC/FABRIC | 188 | $6.50 _____ |
| | Vol. 2 | "Memories In My Heart" by Diane Richards..AC/FABRIC | 189 | $6.50 _____ |
| | Vol. 3 | "Forever In My Heart II" by Diane Richards...AC/FABRIC | 205 | $7.50 _____ |
| | Vol. 5 | "Memories In Your Heart" by Diane Richards | 237 | $7.50 _____ |
| | Vol. 6 | "Angels In My Stocking" by Diane Richards | 254 | $7.50 _____ |
| | Vol. 7 | "Nostalgic Dreams" by Diane Richards | 273 | $8.50 _____ |
| NEW* | Vol. 1 | "Second Time Around" by Sally Sauermilch | 297 | $8.50 _____ |
| | Vol. 1 | "Creations in Canvas...and More" by Carol Spooner | 256 | $7.50 _____ |
| NEW* | Vol. 1 | "Gran's Garden" by Ros Stallcup | 295 | $8.50 _____ |
| | Vol. 1 | "Christmas Visions" by Max Terry | 278 | $8.50 _____ |
| NEW* | Vol. 2 | "Christmas Presence" by Max Terry | 285 | $8.50 _____ |
| | Vol. 1 | "Country Primitives" by Maxine Thomas | 274 | $8.50 _____ |
| | Vol. 1 | "Rise and Shine" by Jolene Thompson | 214 | $6.50 _____ |
| | Vol. 2 | "Garden Gate" by Jolene Thompson | 250 | $7.50 _____ |
| | Vol. 1 | "Count Your Blessings" by Chris Thornton | 176 | $8.50 _____ |
| | Vol. 3 | "Count Your Blessings" by Chris Thornton | 196 | $6.50 _____ |
| | Vol. 5 | "Count Your Blessings" by Chris Thornton | 213 | $8.50 _____ |
| | Vol. 6 | "Share Your Blessings" by Chris Thornton | 226 | $8.50 _____ |
| | Vol. 7 | "Blessings" by Chris Thornton | 255 | $8.50 _____ |
| | Vol. 8 | "Christmas Blessings" by Chris Thornton | 266 | $8.50 _____ |
| | Vol. 9 | "Blessings For The Home" by Chris Thornton | 275 | $8.50 _____ |
| NEW* | Vol.10 | "Bazaar Blessings" by Chris Thornton | 299 | $8.50_____ |
| | Vol. 5 | "Daydreams & Sweet Shirts II" by Don & Lynn Weed | 208 | $7.50 _____ |
| | Vol. 1 | "Floral Fabrics and Watercolor" by Sally Williams | 262 | $8.50 _____ |
| | Vol. 1 | "Friendship Garden" by Shirley Wingert | 253 | $8.50 _____ |

## WATERCOLOR BOOKS

| | | | | |
|---|---|---|---|---|
| | Vol. 20 | "Simply Country Watercolors" by Susan Scheewe | 257 | $8.50 _____ |
| | Vol. 21 | "Simply Watercolor" by Susan Scheewe...TV Book | 260 | $11.95 _____ |
| | Vol. 22 | "Watercolor For Everyone" by Susan Scheewe...T.V. Book | 276 | $11.95 _____ |
| NEW* | Vol. 23 | "Watercolor Step by Step" by Susan Scheewe Brown..T.V...Book | 294 | $11.95 _____ |
| | Vol. 4 | "Enjoy Watercolor" by Ellie Cook | 210 | $7.50 _____ |
| | Vol. 6 | "Watercolor Memories" by Ellie Cook | 246 | $8.50 _____ |
| NEW* | Vol. 7 | "My Favorite Things in Watercolor" by Ellie Cook | 293 | $8.50 _____ |
| | Vol. 1 | "The Way I Started" by Gary Hawk | 120 | $6.00 _____ |
| | Vol. 2 | "Anyone Can Watercolor" by Ken Johnston | 118 | $6.50 _____ |
| | Vol. 1 | "Watercolor Fun and Easy" by Beverly Kaiser | 243 | $7.50 _____ |

*******

**SHIPPING & HANDLING CHARGES**

Add $2.00 for the First Book for shipping and handling.

Add $1.50 per each additional book.

Please Add $3.00 for handling& postage, PER TAPE. Sorry we must have a "NO REFUND-NO RETURN " policy.

U.S. CURRENCY

PRICES SUBJECT TO CHANGE WITHOUT NOTICE

***WE ACCEPT VISA & MASTERCARD***

*Rev.4-13-94*

*13435 N.E. Whitaker Way Portland, Or. 97230 PH (503) 254-9100 FAX (503) 252-9508*